To Nathalie

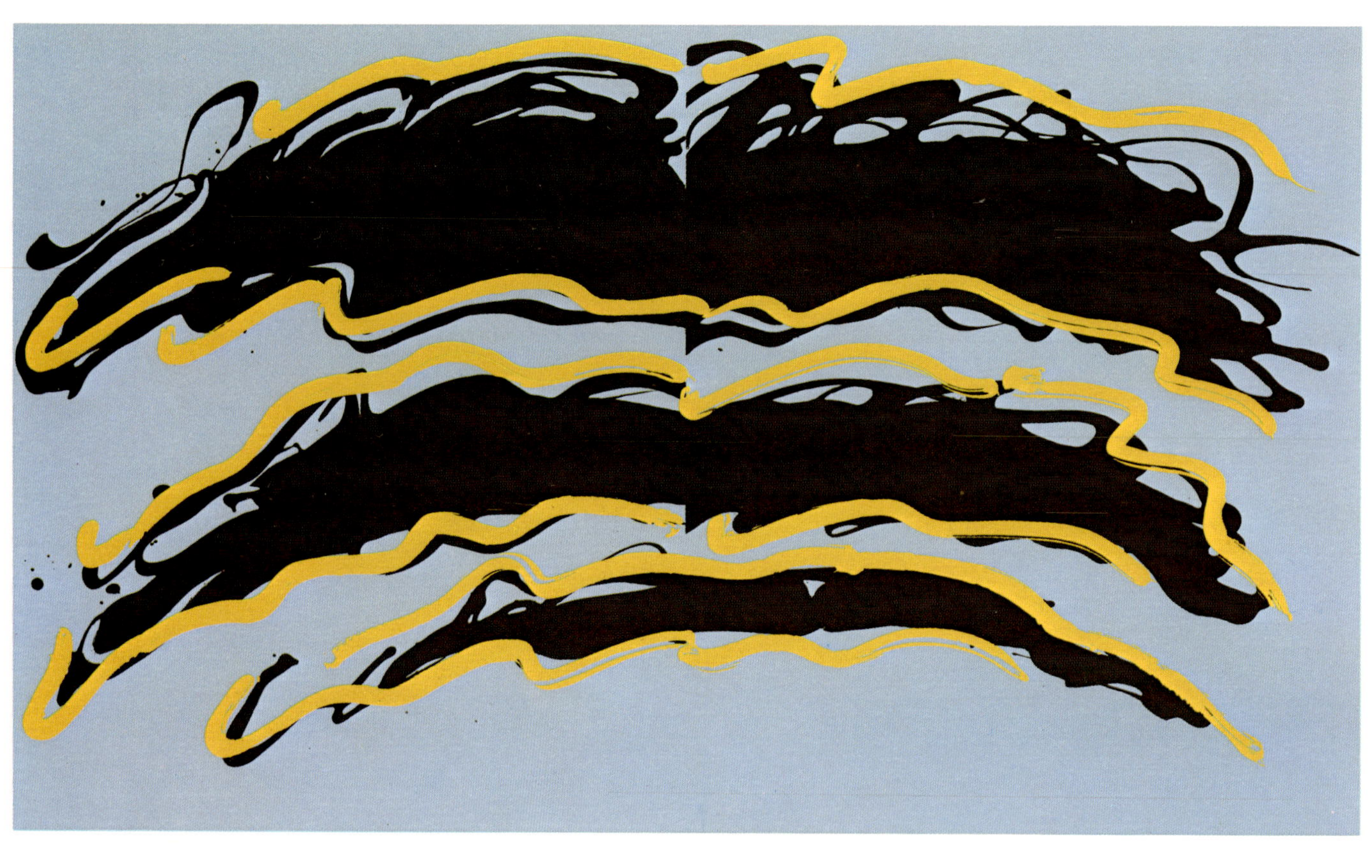

**16** *Long Beach,* 1980

February 9–March 15, 1981

The Art Museum and Galleries
California State University, Long Beach

Mary-Venner Shee

# JACQUES HURTUBISE

## Recent Works
## Oeuvres Récentes

**Exhibition Itinerary**

The Art Museum and Galleries
California State University, Long Beach, California
February 9–March 15, 1981

Canadian Cultural Centre, Canadian Embassy/Centre Culturel
Canadien, Ambassade du Canada, Paris
April 3–May 31, 1981

Sponsored in London by Canada House, Canadian High
Commission/Haut Commissariat du Canada
Summer 1981

Centre Culturel et d'information, Canadian Embassy/
Ambassade du Canada, Brussels
October–December 1981

Art Gallery of Nova Scotia, Halifax
January 4–February 12, 1982


LC 81-33
ISBN 0-936270-16-0
This exhibition has been made possible through the cooperation of the CSULB Associated Students, School of Fine Arts
and the Museum Studies Certificate Program in the Department of Art.
A portion of our general operating funds for this fiscal year has
been made available through a grant from the Institute of
Museum Services, a Federal Agency in The Department of
Education, which offers operating and program support to the
nation's museums.

Cover: Cat. No. 5, *Texite,* 1978



**Library of Congress Cataloging in Publication Data**
Shee, Mary-Venner, 1951–
    Jacques Hurtubise, recent works/oeuvres récentes.
    Catalog of an exhibition.
    Bibliography: p. 48
    1. Hurtubise, Jacques, 1939–      —Exhibitions.
I. California State University, Long Beach. Art Museum and
Galleries. II. Title.
ND249.H88A4   1981   759.11   81.33
ISBN 0-936270-16-0

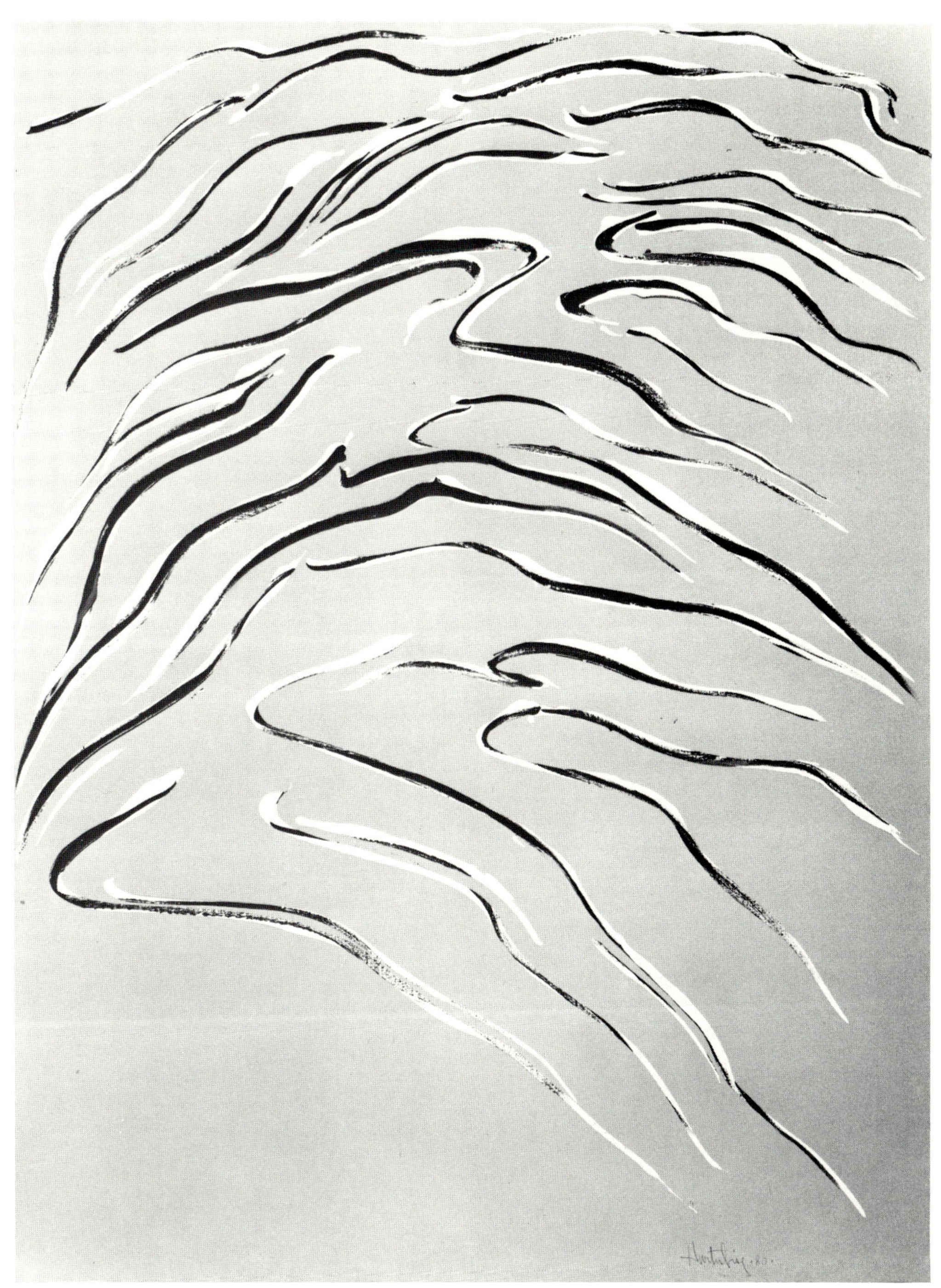

12  *Taflanelle*, 1979

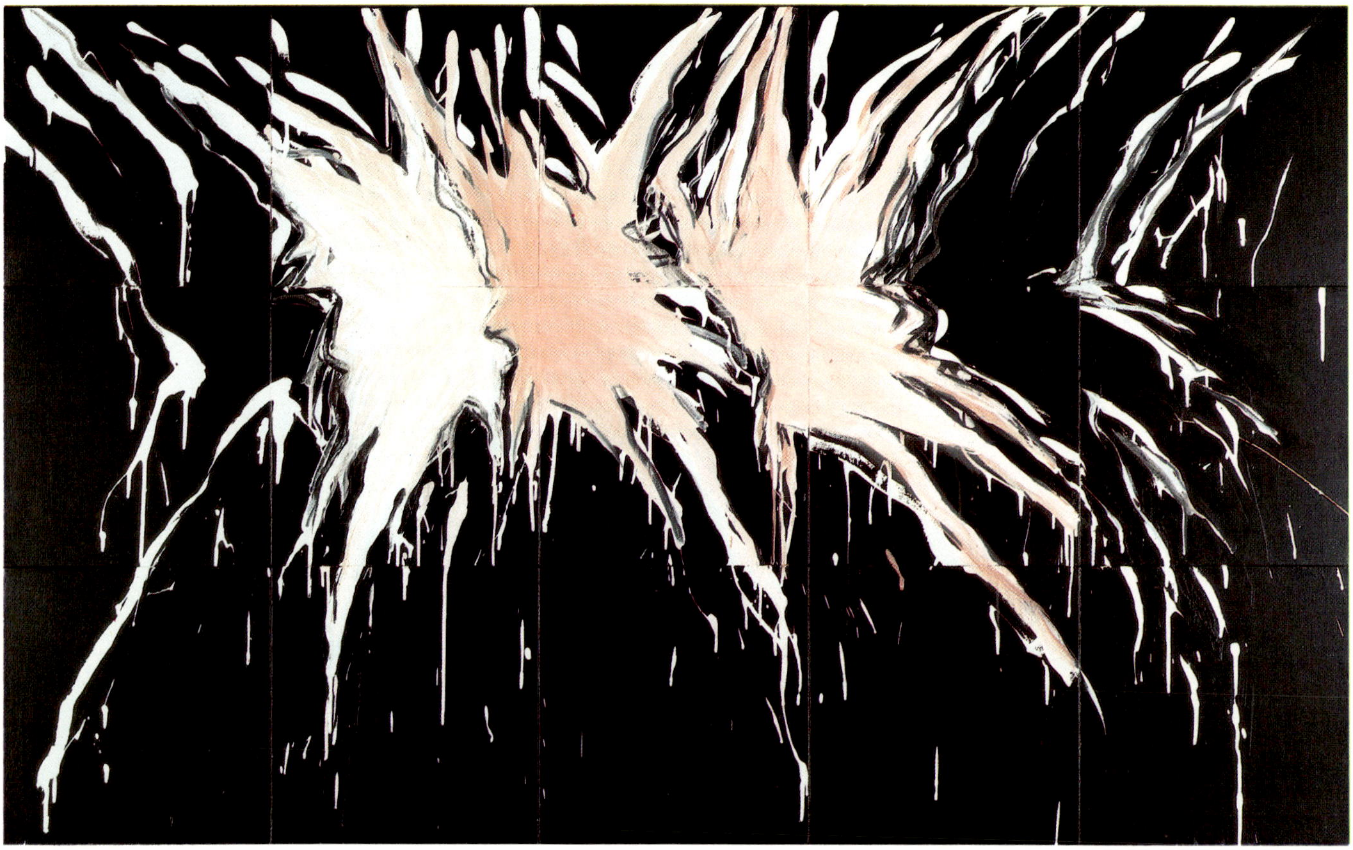

6

**3** *Tatacouna*, 1977

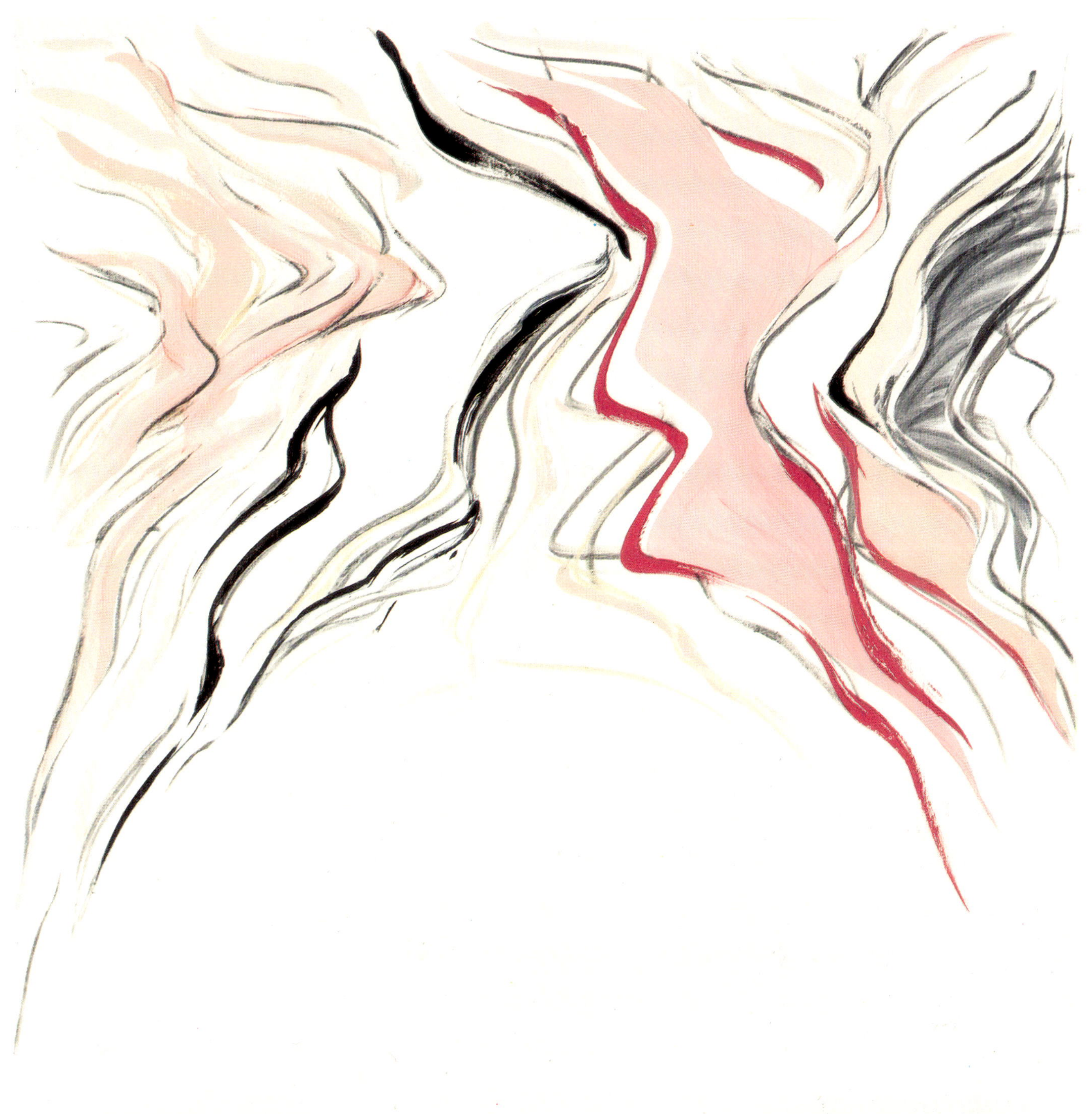



**4** *Tawakiki,* 1978

Nearly two years ago I proposed that the Art Museum and Galleries, California State University, Long Beach sponsor an exhibition of contemporary Canadian art, thus offering a unique opportunity to present works which, although well known in Canada, might be unfamiliar to the Southern California community. The enthusiastic response and counsel I received from Constance Glenn and Jane Bledsoe served to shape the development and final realization of this exhibition.

Upon returning to my home in Quebec, I began investigating the multiplicity of choices open to the University for such an exhibition. The extensive contemporary collection of Mr. and Mrs. Patrick Drouin proved instrumental to the process, for it was in the collection that I first saw the work of Jacques Hurtubise. Well known in Canada, Hurtubise's art had evolved through the various developmental stages common to many French Canadian artists. Thus, although his work was of interest for the commentary it offered on the course of Canadian painting over the past twenty years, the real attraction of the artist lay in the continued intensity of his artistic search which placed his work within the context of international excellence.

Funding for the project was, of course, an essential concern from the beginning. Mr. André Guimond, Cultural Advisor for the Délégation du Québec in Los Angeles agreed to sponsor the project. The Delegation's early involvement stimulated the assistance and participation of other interested institutions and corporations. Recognition is also due Dr. Peter C. Swann, Director of the Samuel and Saidye Bronfman Family Foundation for arranging funding for the exhibition. Additional aspects of this project were orchestrated by Maurice Jodoin in Montreal who carefully oversaw numerous details and provided constant advice, and William Haifley of the CSULB Foundation who administered the funds generated for this exhibition. *Vie Des Arts,* under the directorship of Andrée Paradis, supported this project as part of its ongoing dedication to gaining recognition for Canadian artists at home and abroad. I thank them all, as well as the individual sponsors who believed in the exhibition, in particular Hélène Touzel and Christiane Talbot, who, throughout the summer of 1980, solicited contributions from Quebec corporations.

The essay for this catalogue was drawn from interviews with Hurtubise, Michel Giroux of Galerie Jolliet, Pierre Hamelin, professor of Visual Arts at Laval University in Quebec, and from various newspaper and magazine articles. I owe a debt of gratitude to the writers and critics who have documented the work and exhibitions of Canadian artists for many years. Without them the ideas and perspectives of twentieth century Canadian art would have been lost. Many people were involved in finalizing the text and I extend my sincere thanks to Margaret Whyte, Katia Oliver and Isabelle Baertschi, who gave essential assistance in translating the text; to Robert Thibaudeau, Joan Hemphill, Kathy Huffman and Pauline Cotnoir who aided in the preparation of the manuscript, and to René Viau who contributed his thoughtful insights by sharing material relative to Jacques Hurtubise's artistic evolution.

In addition, special thanks are due Martin McMullen, Alan Holoubek and Bill David Miller who aided with the installation; Jane Bledsoe who, in addition to editing the essay, offered indispensable help in resolving the numerous and exacting details of producing this catalogue; Constance Glenn, for her trustworthy advice, her support and encouragement throughout the project; Gloria Skovronsky who assisted me, not only with administrative tasks, but with the circulation for the exhibition—as a result of her efforts, *Jacques Hurtubise: Recent Works* will circulate through France, Britain, Belgium and Nova Scotia—; and Ann Calhoun, who tirelessly refined the manuscript and whose unfailing good humor, advice and support often fortified my resolve.

It is with deep appreciation and respect that I acknowledge the support and love offered by my mother, Mrs. Edgar Venner Shee, as well as that of Mr. Pierre Vézina, Arthur and Lélia Bousquet and Mrs. Magdeleine H. Simard, all of whom believed in this exhibition from its inception and provided me with unfailing encouragement.

And above all, I extend heart-felt gratitude to Jacques Hurtubise, to his wife Monique, who helped me prepare the bibliography and to their late daughter, Nathalie, who so graciously responded to my every inquiry. It is they who have made this exhibition possible.

**Mary-Venner Shee**


The generous cooperation and expertise of many people have made this exhibition possible and I add my personal thanks to those expressed elsewhere in this catalogue. I am indeed grateful to the many sponsors and patrons both in the United States and in Canada; to the artist for his gifts of time, energy and faith in our endeavors; to the Museum staff for its extraordinary dedication; and finally to Mary-Venner Shee for creating—in partial fulfillment of the requirements for the Master of Arts Degree in Museology and Education—a noteworthy exhibit which is exemplary of exchanges we too seldom pursue with our counterparts in Quebec, Canada and abroad. The Museum is proud to support Mary's graduate work and to provide the first presentation of Hurtubise's work in California and the West.

**Constance W. Glenn,** *Director*



# ACKNOWLEDGEMENTS

We wish to gratefully acknowledge the assistance of the following corporations and individuals; without their generous support, this exhibition would not have been possible./ Nous tenons à remercier les institutions et les personnes qui ont participé à ce projet, sans leur aide cette exposition n'aurait pu être possible.

P. E. Bousquet Inc., Terrebonne
The Samuel and Saidye Bronfman Family Foundation, Montreal
La Caisse Populaire Desjardins de Sillery
Canadian Consulate General/Consulat Général du Canada, Los Angeles
Galerie Jolliet, Quebec
Marcel Lacroix, Inc., Quebec
Mercier/Ouimet/Masse, Inc., Montreal
Ministère des Affaires Culturelles du Québec, Aide à la Création
Ministère des Affaires Intergouvernementales du Québec, Délégation du Québec, Los Angeles
Rémy-Martin
Ruel et Frères Ltée.,/Ruel Bros. Ltd, Levis
Sodarcan, inc., Montreal
Tassé & Associés Ltée., Montreal
*Vie Des Arts,* Quarterly Art Magazine, Montreal
Mrs. Monique G. Barry, Quebec
Mr. and Mrs. Euclide Bisson, Quebec
Mr. and Mrs. Arthur Bousquet, Ottawa
Mr. and Mrs. Lucien Boulet, Quebec
Mr. and Mrs. Jean Brochu, Quebec
Mrs. Danielle Civitella, Quebec
Mr. and Mrs. Patrice Fleury, Quebec
Mr. and Mrs. Jean A. Gagné, Quebec
Mr. and Mrs. Robert Garneau, Quebec
Mr. and Mrs. Yves Gauthier, Montreal
Mr. Jules Gauvin, Quebec
Mr. Pierre Gendron, Quebec
Mr. and Mrs. Michel Guay, Quebec
Mr. and Mrs. Maurice Jodoin, Montreal
Mrs. Guy Lebrun, Quebec
Mrs. Magdelon Garneau Monast, Montreal
Mrs. Carmen Morin, Quebec
Mr. and Mrs. Eric Morisette, Quebec
Mr. and Mrs. Jean-Paul Parent, Quebec
Mrs. France Gagnon Pratte, Quebec
Mr. and Mrs. Anatole Robichaud, Quebec
Mr. and Mrs. Jean-Louis Rousseau, Quebec
Mrs. Edgar Venner Shee, Quebec
Ms. Sandra Shee, Quebec
Mrs. Paul M. A. Simard, Quebec
Mr. Jean Turcotte, Quebec
Mr. Pierre Vézina, Quebec

University Art Museums are responsible to an aesthetic duality, academic enrichment which demands a representative art historical program and scholarly pursuits which prompt the investigation of art and artists not yet accorded a place in text books. *Jacques Hurtubise: Recent Works* happily fulfills both needs. Hurtubise is fully an artist of his time, reflecting in his works a concomitant examination of the artistic concerns prevalent throughout the past twenty-five years in the United States as well as Canada. At the same time his work is relatively unfamiliar to museum and gallery patrons outside his native country. Regrettably Canadian artists are often not as well known in the United States as their counterparts in other regions of North America, not from a lack of aesthetic vigor but rather from the absence of a forum for their works. A parallel situation is often lamented by American artists who choose not to work in New York.

Students, faculty, staff and visitors to CSULB have been fortunate in the past few years to have had the opportunity to become aware of the work of three Canadian artists. Robert Murray and Rita Letendre were two of eight participants in the International Sculpture Symposium in 1965 and their works, *Duet* and *Sunrise,* have become integral elements in the campus visual milieu. In addition, sculptor Robert Downing taught studio classes for several semesters in the mid 1970s and was included in two faculty exhibitions. Downing's sculpture addresses many of the same concerns for geometric order which he, like Hurtubise, may have adopted from the *Plasticiens*.

The present exhibition is, however, the first in which a comprehensive examination of the work of a Canadian artist has been organized for this campus. Following the Long Beach opening, the exhibit is scheduled to travel in Europe and Canada before returning to the United States for additional engagements. The Art Museum and Galleries is pleased to be a part of this exhibition, to have played a role in facilitating the development and realization of the exhibition concept by curator Mary-Venner Shee, herself a native of Quebec, whom we at CSULB have had the great fortune to come to know and respect as a connoisseur and art historian. Her dedication to this project has resulted in an exhibition which will serve, through this catalogue, to record a segment of international art history as well as provide a critically prepared presentation of the recent paintings and prints of Jacques Hurtubise for audiences outside of Canada.

In addition to my personal gratitude to Mary Shee for her efforts, I wish to thank and acknowledge the artist, the many contributors, and the gallery staff for their generosity and cooperation which have made this exhibition possible.

**Jane K. Bledsoe,** *Administrative Director*



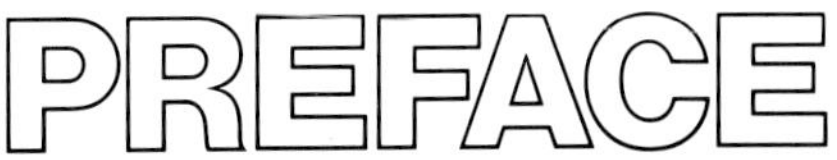

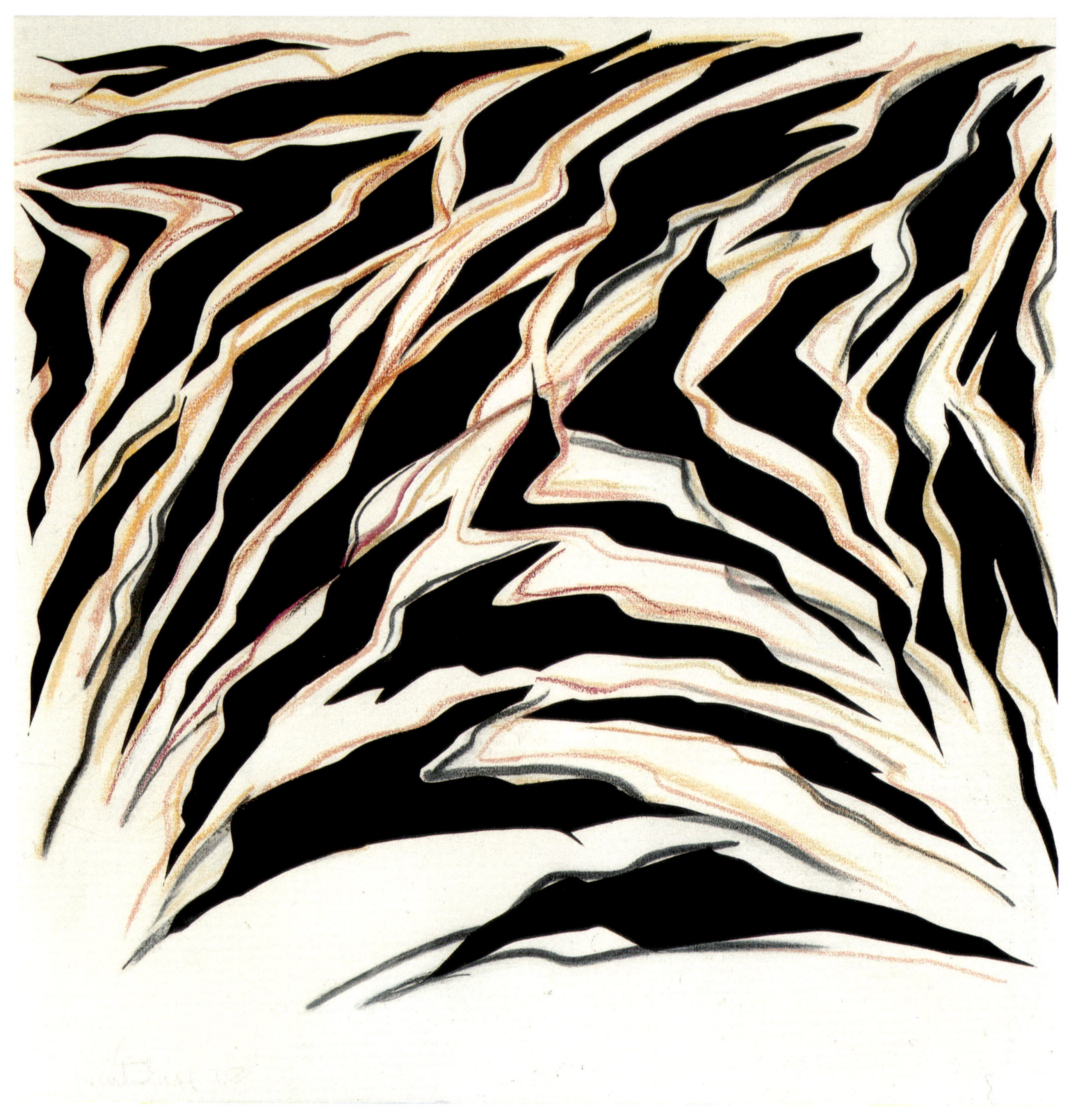

10

**6** *Taniwaki,* 1978

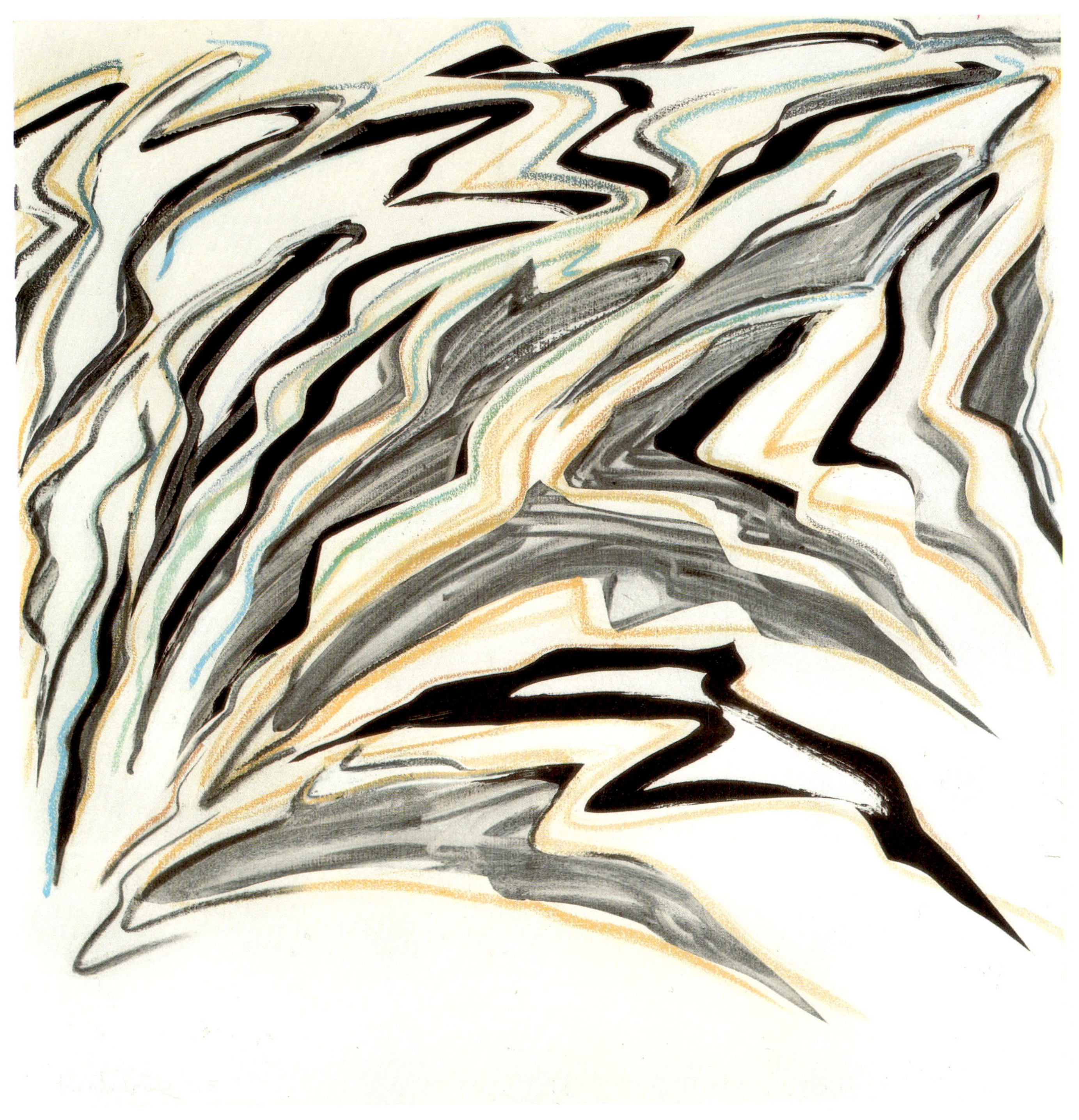



**7**  *Tawapitie,* 1978

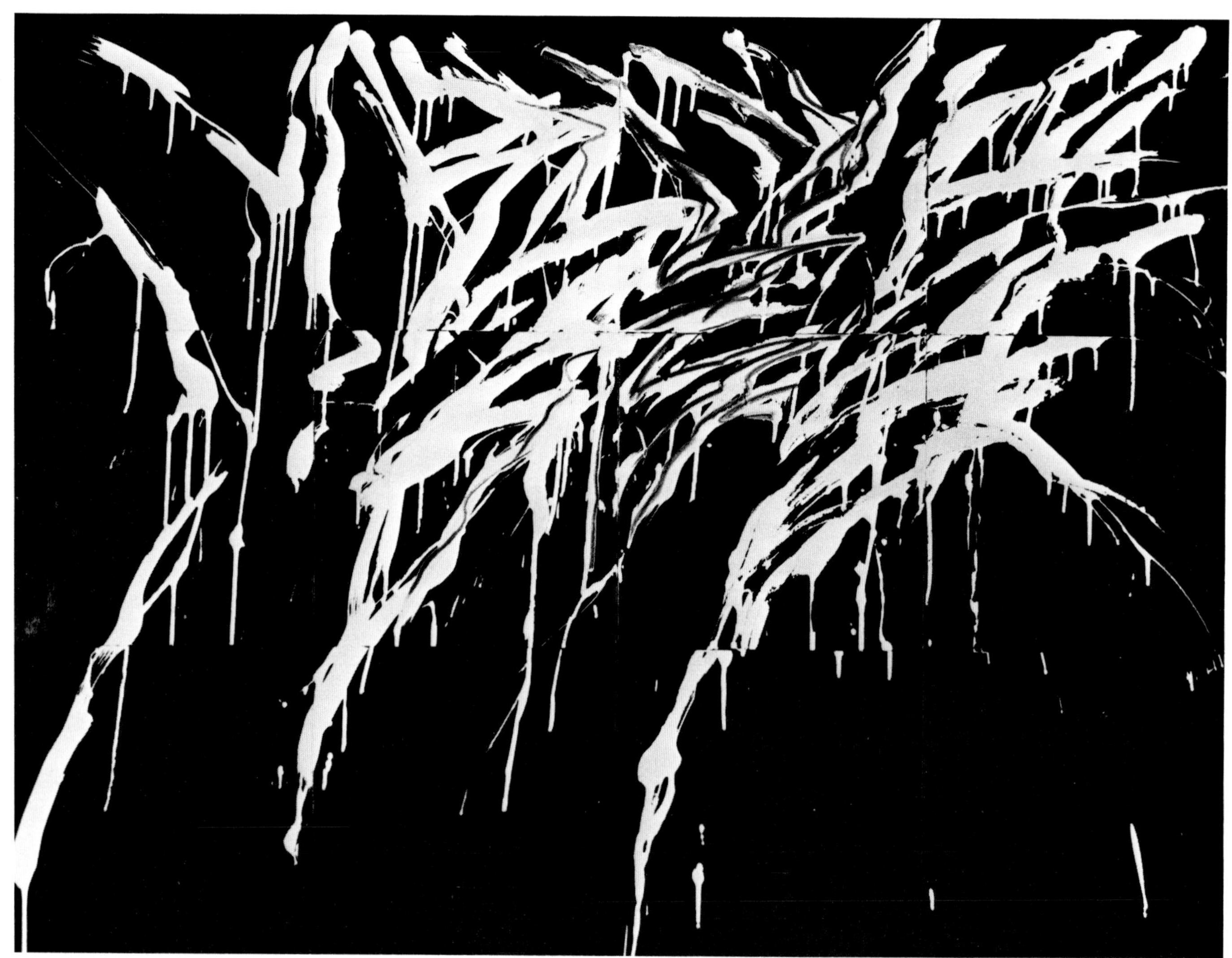

12

**2** *Tapéribonka,* 1977

*Text figures are on pages 18 and 19.*

*Although Hurtubise has been strongly influenced by American Abstract Expressionism, he has developed his style as a synthesis and an amalgam of currents which have been influential in Quebec for the past twenty years. For Hurtubise the gesture becomes form. Far from being an autobiographical projection and a tribute to expressionism, Hurtubise's painting is today a complex ensemble of planes and lines creating a convex space, organized through the juxtaposition of waves based upon the subtle radiation of color. The ambiguity of background and surface persists reinforcing the "toppling effect" of these disarming, oblique paintings....*

Excerpted from an unpublished essay by René Viau

The art of Jacques Hurtubise and the personality of the man are, in the tradition of Abstract Expressionism, interwoven in a deep-seated unity. Through the language of color and form, the artist gives expression to his inner drives, his instincts, his pains and his pleasures, simultaneously experiencing the exhilaration of total freedom and the exhaustion of total surrender. His art is gestural, visceral and violent, perhaps tending to stun rather than attract the viewer, but without the heavy impasto surface often associated with art of this genre. Gilles Toupin said of him, *"...for Hurtubise, art proceeds from the expression of his own existence...;"*[1] and early in his career, Hurtubise once remarked to the critic, Robert Millet, *"I paint therefore I am."*[2] However, throughout the past twenty-five years his commitment to artistic endeavor has been consistently revealed through his statements about his art and himself:

*When I paint, it is totally engrossing. I do nothing else. I get the feeling that my paintings are my mirror image. The painting and me, face to face, we're just one and the same thing. We're stuck with each other. That's how it is...*[3]

*If you don't like my painting, you don't like me.*[4]

*If I am hungry, I eat; if I am thirsty, I drink; if I want to create a painting I do it as fast as possible. Some people think about their work for ages before starting to paint...*[5]

*I don't have time to stand back and reflect...I think of painting, my mind paints, and I paint.*[6]

*I do my paintings non-stop, two or even three works at a time. When I do stop, it's because I think they're good, they're powerful, and I can't improve on them.*[7]

*I'm always tense when I paint. It's a tremendous strain... For me, smoking is stressful, walking is stressful; but when I work I have to be under an even higher degree of stress, or it's just not possible.*[8]

*Hell, it's a tough profession. It eats up all your energy, and your life as well.*[9]

Hurtubise is generally deemed to have a spontaneous, generous, yet meticulous and severe personality. These traits are reflected in his paintings, which articulate primordial tensions and impulses even while employing a precisely refined and orderly language. Hurtubise's particular synthetic vocabulary is derived from the dialectical opposition of expressionism and geometric formality. As early as 1966, during his New York premiere at Marlborough Gallery, he described himself as a *different* painter and affirmed that it was possible to retain a personal element even in an art form which was becoming increasingly impersonal and universal. Simone Auger, who interviewed him on that occasion, stated:

*There is an aspect of fantasy in his work which puts him in a class by himself; it is neither pure Abstract Expressionism nor pure Hard-Edge. Though art is becoming increasingly impersonal, and even anonymous at times, Hurtubise believes that a personal touch is still possible.*[10]

From the outset of his career, recognition was given to his strength, his determination and the untamed force of his will to work. *"A dialectician, hardworking, high-strung, and prolific. There you have Jacques Hurtubise in a nutshell..."*[11] The paintings in this exhibition, *Jacques Hurtubise: Recent Works,* have been made in the past three years and represent significant changes which have occurred in the artist's work, reflecting Hurtubise's stature as a mature talent. These recent developments cannot, however, be fully understood without an examination of the artist's entire oeuvre. This essay has been drawn from interviews with the artist, as well as from the critical writings of Simone Auger, Richard Crevier, Fernande Saint-Martin and Gilles Toupin, in order that the *Recent Works* can be examined within the context of the artist's own career, as well as the mainstream of contemporary art.

**The Early Years**

*"...I did what everyone else was doing,"*[12] says Hurtubise, describing the figurative works he painted at the *Ecole des Beaux-Arts de Montreal* from 1956 to 1960. The paintings illustrate his assimilation of traditional techniques—canons of proportion and perspective, rules of composition—and his



# JACQUES HURTUBISE:
# RECENT WORKS

concentration on the landscapes and scenes around the old Port of Montreal, (fig. 1 *Le Port,* 1957). His first group exhibition took place at the Hélène de Champlain Restaurant, an avant-garde exhibit space for young artists on Montreal's St. Helen's Island, in 1957 while he was still enrolled at the School. Pierre Saucier said of him then:

> *Jacques Hurtubise has a refined technique. He has a highly developed sense of movement. His landscape of burned trees has the delicate style of the Japanese. Colour is muted, and thinned down like a leafless fall scene. Slender, bare, delicate trunks rise against a blue, pink and white sky, bathed with a soft melancholy charm.*[13]

A 1958 painting, *Sentier,* won public acclaim at the 75th Annual Spring Exhibition at the Montreal Museum of Fine Arts.

In late 1960, he received a grant from the Max Beckman Foundation and left Quebec to spend eight months in New York where he became familiar with the art of Jackson Pollock, Franz Kline and Willem de Kooning. This exposure to new ideas and the expression of immediate feeling in painting affected Hurtubise as it did many younger painters, and he has noted that his work took a new direction from that moment.[14] *Radioactivité No. 4,* 1961 (fig. 2), is the most representative of these works, illustrating the new primacy which he accorded free gesture. This composition suggests both the traditional integrity of space considered as depth and the ambiguity which resulted from the equalization of figure-ground relationships. As Hurtubise explored the manipulation of color and form, which was characteristic of Abstract Expressionism, his compositions became filled with loosely painted masses. However, he was uncomfortable with the lack of structure he felt to be inherent in Abstract Expressionism and began searching for a means to combine gesture and movement within a systematic format. He began to solve this problem by sectioning the pictorial space into large ragged areas of color which he juxtaposed, superimposed and elongated into drip-like forms.

This search for order led him to a group called the *Plasticiens.* These Montreal artists organized in the mid 1950s to advocate a formalist approach employing geometric configurations, symmetry and serial repetition, in reaction to the "action painting" movement led in Quebec by Paul-Emile Borduas. The formal rigidity promoted by the *Plasticiens* corresponded to Hurtubise's need for structure and he adopted this portion of their idiom and combined it with the gestural spontaneity of Abstract Expressionism. This synthesis is most clearly revealed in the 1964 work, *Quadrature* (fig. 3). Toupin noted:

> *By a blending of the concepts of geometrism and the splash, the painting forms an entity that conveys at one and the same time a duality, order and chaos, within the same space.*[15]

## 1964—A Turning Point: The Splash and Hard Edge

Hurtubise, in 1964, introduced a third idiom into his work. In addition to the gestural characteristics of Abstract Expressionism and the geometric organization and serial imagery of the *Plasticiens,* he now began to employ techniques of the Hard-Edge School, namely flat surfaces and clearly rendered edges. Characteristic of these works was a newly refined motif Toupin referred to as the "splash." In his introduction to an exhibition at the Galerie du Siecle in 1966, Richard Crevier described the splash as *"The spontaneous flow itself,...the double value of an object on a background and of a foreground on a space."*[16] Although the splash appeared as a form which had exploded on a flat background, close examination reveals it to be a motif which was systematically reduced to an intrinsic, anonymous shape which he integrated into his geometric style. Repeated and reversed in mirror images on a system of axes, it became a formal element that diminished the distinction between field and ground. Fernande Saint-Martin wrote about the 1966 paintings for *Art International:*

> (Hurtubise) *uses an almost mechanical technique of working on the edges of the splash to remove all expressibility and lyricism from it; he wants to prove that a splash is just as "non-expressive" as any standard formal element... the vertical plane is as much a splash element as the splash a plane.*[17]

Hurtubise's selective use of pure vibrant colors increased the tension created by the disappearance of figure-ground definition. This effect became even more pronounced in works such as *Iris,* 1966 (fig. 4). In this painting, the splash becomes a series of shapes, reproduced by means of a stencil, balancing positive and negative space within a geometrically organized structure, creating the impression that pattern and background are reversible. Although apparently closely allied with the then emerging Op Art movement, the forms derived from the previous paintings were consistent with Hurtubise's ongoing search for structural order. Hurtubise also shifted the canvas, which had interchangeable vertical and horizontal planes, to a diagonal orientation. His preoccupation with the technique of eliminating the definition between positive and negative spaces and the optical effects produced by the application of vibrant, contrasting colors during this period predicted the exploration of luminosity which was to begin the following year.

## 1967—The Neons

In 1967 Hurtubise was invited to be artist-in-residence at Dartmouth College in Hanover, New Hampshire, where he painted the works which were to represent Canada at the *IX Biennial* in São Paulo, Brazil. His search for optical luminosity intensified at this time and gave rise to his "light paintings." Later, during an interview with Saint-Martin at his 1973 retrospective at the Montreal Musée d'art contemporian he explained the development of these paintings: *"Before my neon works, my search for light had led me to do paintings that were so luminous they were almost white. Where could I go from there, if not to neon?"*[18]

In an attempt to transcend the limitations imposed by the residual opacity inherent in pigmented mediums, he sought maximum color intensity through the spectrum embodied in neon light. Manipulating neon tubing in a near replication of his linear patterns, placing the complex tubing against a flat black background, he hoped to transcend the limitations of pigment. When Norman Theriault questioned Hurtubise about this new development, the artist replied that he *"used neon lights because you can't get pots of electric paint…As far as I am concerned, my neon works are not sculptures but paintings."*[19] His response indicates that he was transposing a form of expression from one medium to another and that his intent was not to exploit the sculptural qualities normally associated with neon art of the sixties. *Ciboulette,* 1969 (fig. 5) illustrates this concern and establishes that the radical change of medium did not prompt adoption of a new formal language. Although his objective to extend his understanding of luminosity appears to have been well served by his apprenticeship with neon, financial considerations, as well as the exacting technical and physical demands of the material, eventually led Hurtubise to abandon his "light paintings" and return to the more traditional medium of paint on canvas.

## 1970—Equal Squares

By 1970 Hurtubise used the square, a familiar pattern from earlier work often hidden by the use of color and figure-ground relationships, as a more evident device in his compositions. Throughout the 1970s the square was to remain a basic structure and a major element of his style. In an early work of this period, *Marie-Jeanne,* 1970 (fig. 6), diagonal zigzag motifs, as geometrized abstractions of the splash, oppose a delineated grid pattern. Rendered in a free interplay of fluorescent pink, orange, blue and acid green against a dense black background, the broken edges of the pattern move the eye diagonally, emphasizing the lack of distinction between shape and ground. Gradually the artist increased the area of black, which eventually dominated the paintings, leaving a few traces of fluorescent color glittering on the periphery of the grid to add emphasis to the format.

Beginning in 1972, instead of painting a grid upon the canvas, Hurtubise cut the canvas into discrete square modules which he painted individually and then arranged and permanently assembled as completed paintings. Once assembled, the squares ceased to be autonomous elements and became, instead, a coherent composition. He said in an interview with Saint-Martin:

> I was fed up with grid-type structures, modular structures, and the search for subtle chromatic effects. I made radical changes in my working style, in the way I produced my paintings.[20]

Hurtubise abandoned the predetermined grid because of the compositional limits which it imposed. Although using the same format, the square, he nevertheless freed himself from the immediate necessity to organize and compose the entire canvas. Once painted, the movable elements permitted infinite recombination and arrangement until a final composition was realized. Toupin, writing in *La Presse,* described this style as a game: *"…this construction has a connotation of play, for his art is at the level of play, though it is a game that is inextricably bound to the fundamental purpose of his existence, to be an artist."*[21]

Hurtubise continued to employ movable squares for several years, de-emphasizing color as the major dynamic in favor of shapes, contours, dribbles and carefully executed splashes oriented on the diagonal, to create an internal energy suggesting continuation beyond the edges of the canvas. Contrasting colors such as blacks and reds, pinks and yellows, as in *Roxie,* 1974 (fig. 7) emphasize the play of shapes against the background without defining positive and negative space. Everything about these complex paintings is crafted; nothing is left to chance, even though the imagery seems to be free and spontaneous. Hurtubise himself often says that the more spontaneous his paintings seem to be, the more structured they really are. While painting these works, which appear to be gestural and uninhibited, he eliminated all possibility of opportune accident or happenstance by carefully masking even the most irregular and organic edges.

## 1977–1980—The New Direction

The modular paintings culminate in 1977 with *Tapéribonka* and *Tatacouna* (cat. nos. 2 & 3). In these works, which are the earliest included in this exhibition, the arranged squares form paintings that are both a synthesis of previous efforts and the departure point for the development Hurtubise was to pursue in the next two years. In *Tatacouna,* a three splash form dominates the center of the canvas as a flattened shape upon a ground. Radiating from the splashes are linear, gestural strokes. These strokes become the crucial element in subsequent paintings. In two following works, *Tawakiki* and *Texite* (cat. nos. 4 & 5), both produced in 1977, Hurtubise returned to the spontaneous gestural language which he had employed in earlier works such as *Impatience,* 1961 (fig. 8). No longer consisting of flat planar forms occupying ambiguous spaces, these works are instead descriptions of curvilinear volumes and for the first time they present some hint of perspective and distance. Crucial also to recent works is Hurtubise's abandonment of any vestiges of the module or grid as a formal element. Each painting is now a description of a singular topological mass.

In 1978 he refined and simplified the new imagery in works such as *Taniwaki* and *Tawapitie* (cat. nos. 6 & 7) into economically rendered, sharply edged forms suggesting bulging global expanses and spare delineations of landscape-like masses. The forms and the contrast of color to the neutral ground describe linear patterns which create such tensions that the surface of the canvas itself seems to be pulled or warped.

Examination of the balance of the pieces selected for this exhibition reveals imagery which continues these elements of landscape and global volumes. The selected works produced in 1979, *Takarakas* (cat. 8), *Tadoussac* (cat. 9), *Tafarina* (cat. 10), *Taflanelle* (cat. 12) and *Tamarakas* (cat. 13) are characterized by abbreviated stroke-like forms describing undulating masses. Although these paintings still retain the flat, smooth surfaces which have characterized his work since 1964, the depiction of distance is becoming more pronounced. The 1980 works, *Texado* (cat. 14) and *Tazuni* (cat. 15), continue this trend and, in addition, reintroduce surface texture emphasizing the gestural, curvilinear qualities of his imagery through heavier application of paint and the use of pastel and charcoal that provides contrasting color and defines volume.

Although Hurtubise's paintings have progressed through a series of stylistic and technical changes, the dominant factor which emerges, when the totality of his work is examined, is consistency. Remnants of his earliest depictions of the old Port of Montreal emerge throughout his paintings. With his most recent works, which have become less flat and planar, carrying a suggestion of topographic illusionism—echoes of the earth's surface—the artist has come full circle and is again rendering descriptions which, although lacking organic specificity, nonetheless indeed depict the landscape in its most abstract form.

**Mary-Venner Shee**

[1] Gilles Toupin, "Ces tableaux à noms de femmes," *La Presse* (Montreal), 10 February 1973, sec. D, p. 14.

[2] Robert Millet, "Jacques Hurtubise: Je peins donc je suis!" *Le Magazine Maclean* (Montreal), February 1969, p. 55.

[3] Pierre Pelletier, "Jacques Hurtubise, peintre," *Le Droit* (Ottawa), 30 April 1977, p. 18.

[4] Gilles Toupin, "Hurtubise et les transes de l'Amérique," *La Presse* (Montreal), 26 October 1974, sec. E, p. 19.

[5] Millet, "Jacques Hurtubise: Je peins donc je suis!" p. 55.

[6] Pelletier, "Jacques Hurtubise, peintre," p. 18.

[7] Toupin, "Hurtubise et les transes de l'Amérique," p. 19.

[8] Pelletier, "Jacques Hurtubise, peintre," p. 18.

[9] Toupin, "Hurtubise et les transes de l'Amérique," p. 19.

[10] Simone Auger, "Hurtubise: Quand on a réussi à Montréal, on n'est pas rendu bien loin," *La Presse* (Montreal), 16 July 1966, p. 13.

[11] Millet, "Hurtubise vers l'abstraction," *Le Magazine Maclean* (Montreal), February 1962, p. 53.

[12] Auger, "Hurtubise: Quand on a réussi à Montréal...," p. 13.

[13] Pierre Saucier, "Les promesses artistiques de demain à Hélène de Champlain," *La Patrie* (Montreal), 24 November 1957, p. 130.

[14] Auger, "Hurtubise: Quand on a réussi à Montréal...," p. 13.

[15] Toupin, "Ces tableaux à noms de femmes," p. 14.

[16] Richard Crevier, *Jacques Hurtubise.* (Montreal: Galerie du Siècle Inc., 1966), n. pag.

[17] Fernande Saint-Martin, "Lettre de Montréal, Jacques Hurtubise," *Art International,* February 1966, p. 47.

[18] Saint-Martin, "Jacques Hurtubise," *Atelier* (Montreal), February 1973, pp. 1–2.

[19] Normand Thériault, "Hurtubise 'je suis instinctif,'" *La Presse* (Montreal), 25 October 1969, p. 39.

[20] Saint-Martin, "Jacques Hurtubise," pp. 1–2.

[21] Toupin, "Hurtubise et les transes de l'Amérique," p. 19.

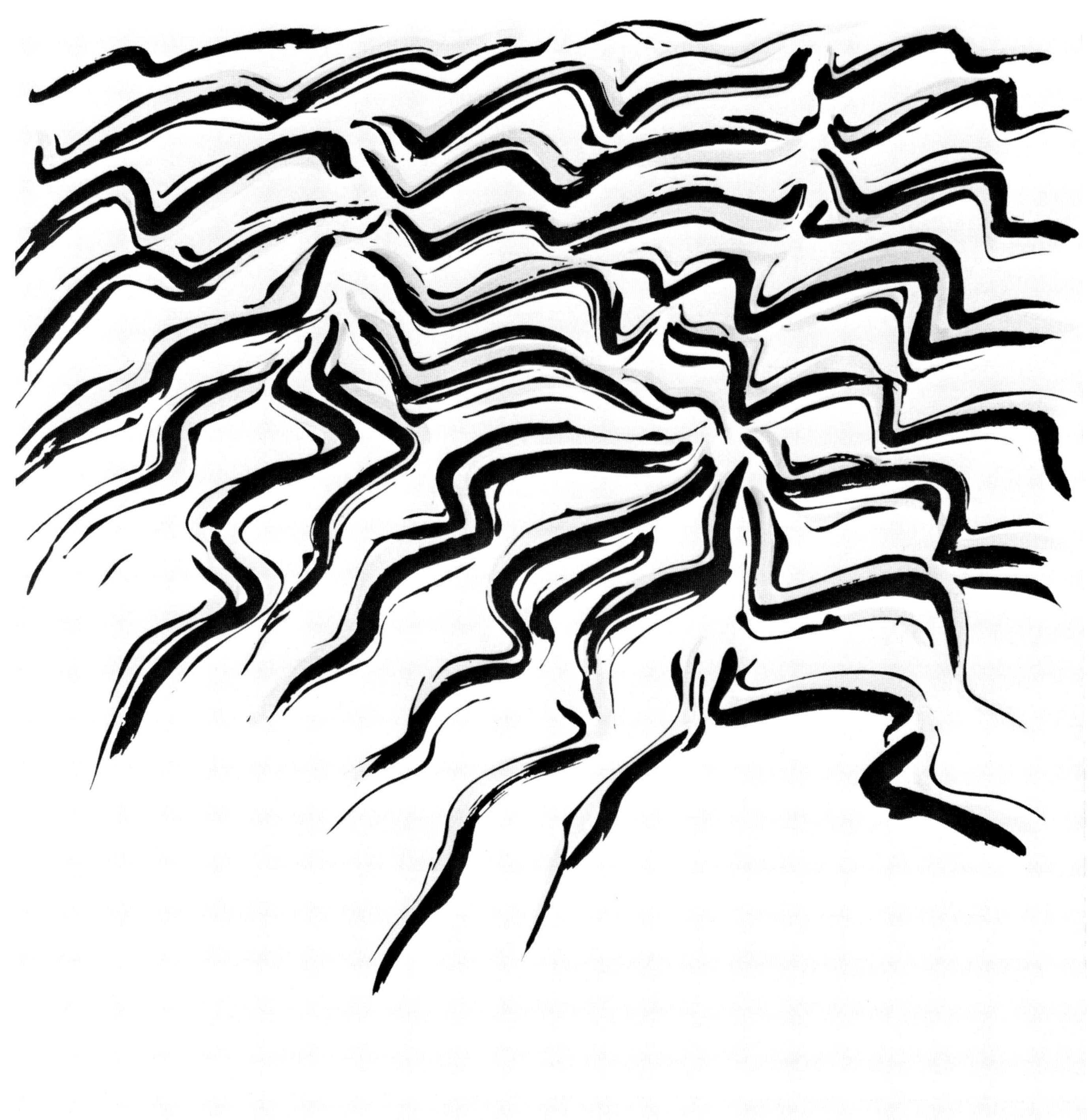

11 *Tavanille,* 1979

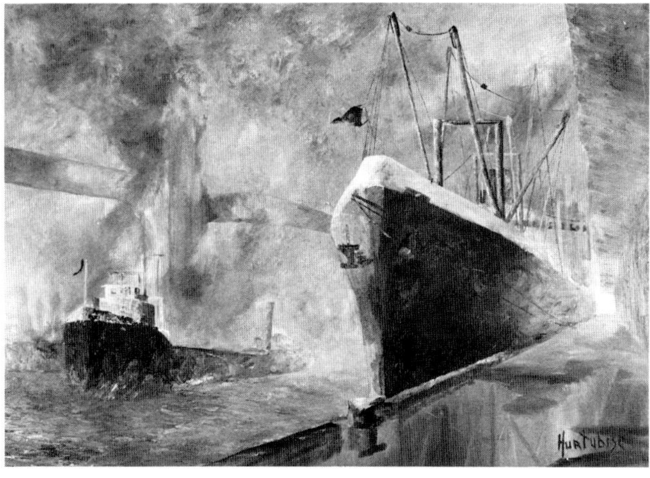

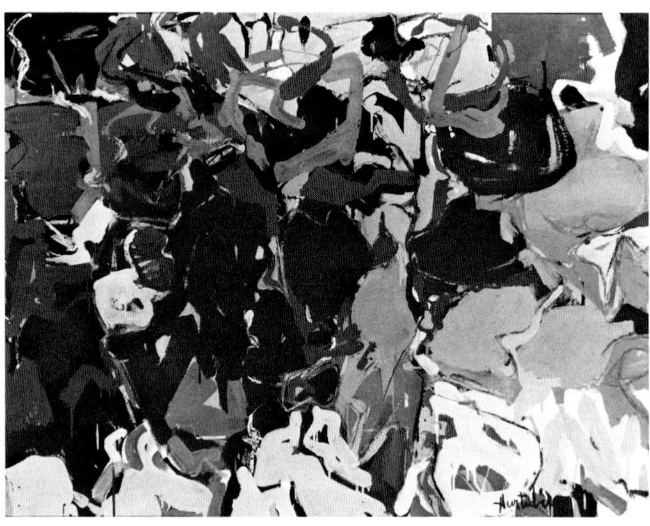

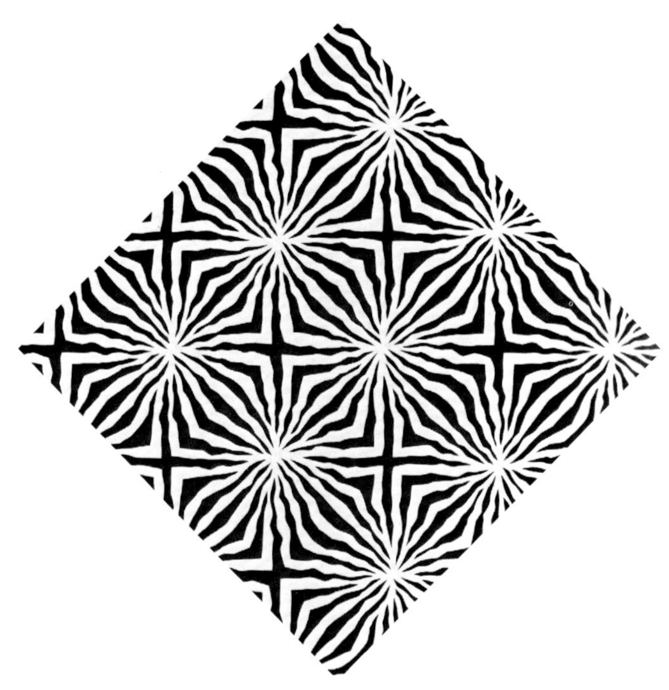

18

Fig. 1 *Le Port*, 1957
Oil on canvas/Huile sur toile
25 x 30 (63.5 x 76.2)

Fig. 2 *Radioactivité No. 4*, 1961
Enamel, charcoal and pastel on Masonite/Email, fusain et
pastel sur Masonite
36 x 48 (91.4 x 121.9)

Fig. 3 *Quadrature*, 1964
Acrylic on paper/Acrylique sur papier
24 x 20 (61 x 50.8)
Collection of Monique Colangelo, Terrebonne

Fig. 4 *Iris*, 1966
Acrylic on canvas/Acrylique sur toile
67 x 67 (170.2 x 170.2)

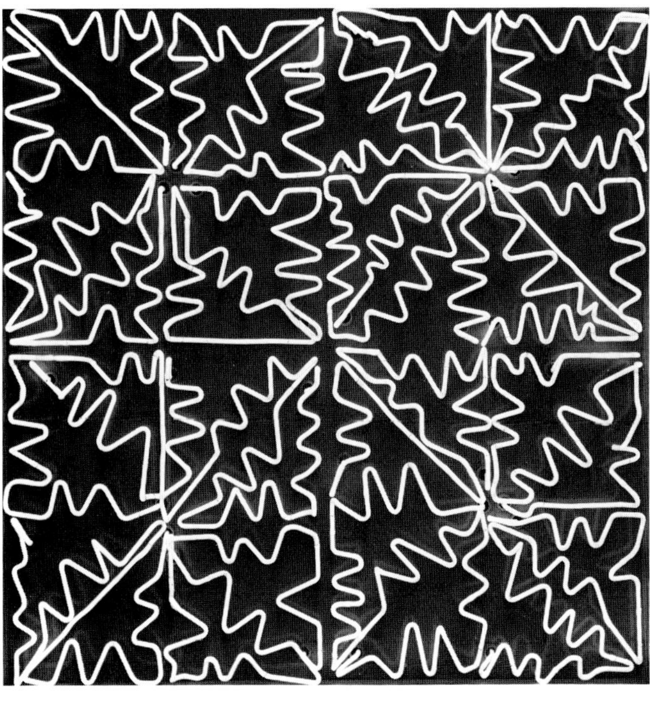

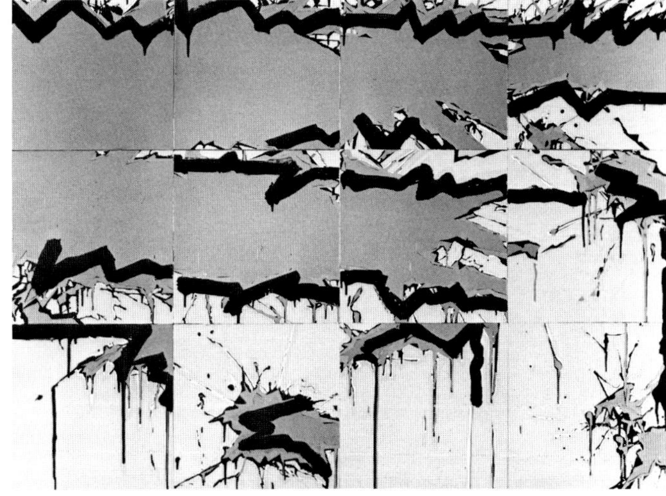

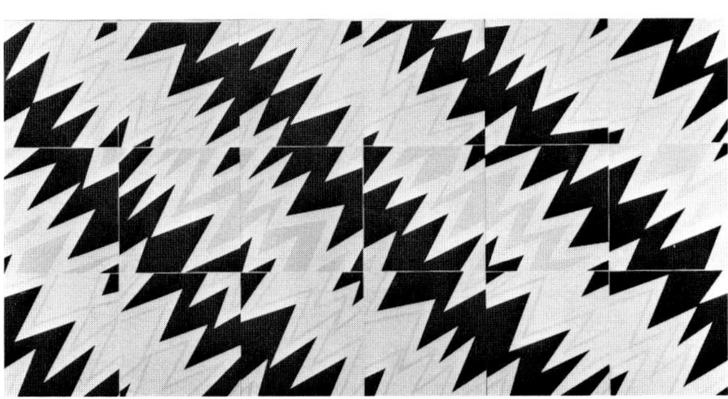

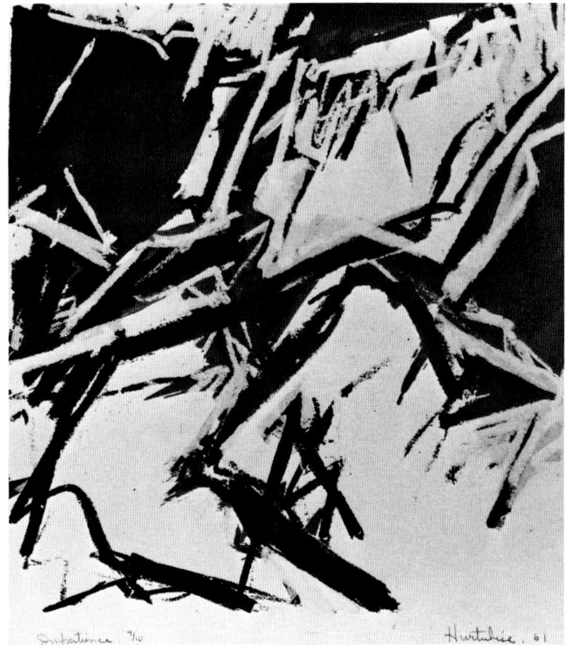



Fig. 5  *Ciboulette*, 1968
Neon tubing and steel/Tubes de néon et acier
80 x 80 x 18 (203.2 x 203.2 x 45.7)
Collection of Musée d'art contemporain, Montreal

Fig. 6  *Marie-Jeanne*, 1970
Acrylic on canvas/Acrylique sur toile
99 x 198 (251.5 x 503)
Collection of the Confederation Center Art Gallery and Museum,
Charlottetown, Prince Edward Island

Fig. 7  *Roxie*, 1974
Acrylic on canvas/Acrylique sur toile
48 x 64 (121.9 x 162.6)

Fig. 8  *Impatience*, 1961
Serigraph/Serigraphie 7/10
18½ x 17 (47 x 43.2)

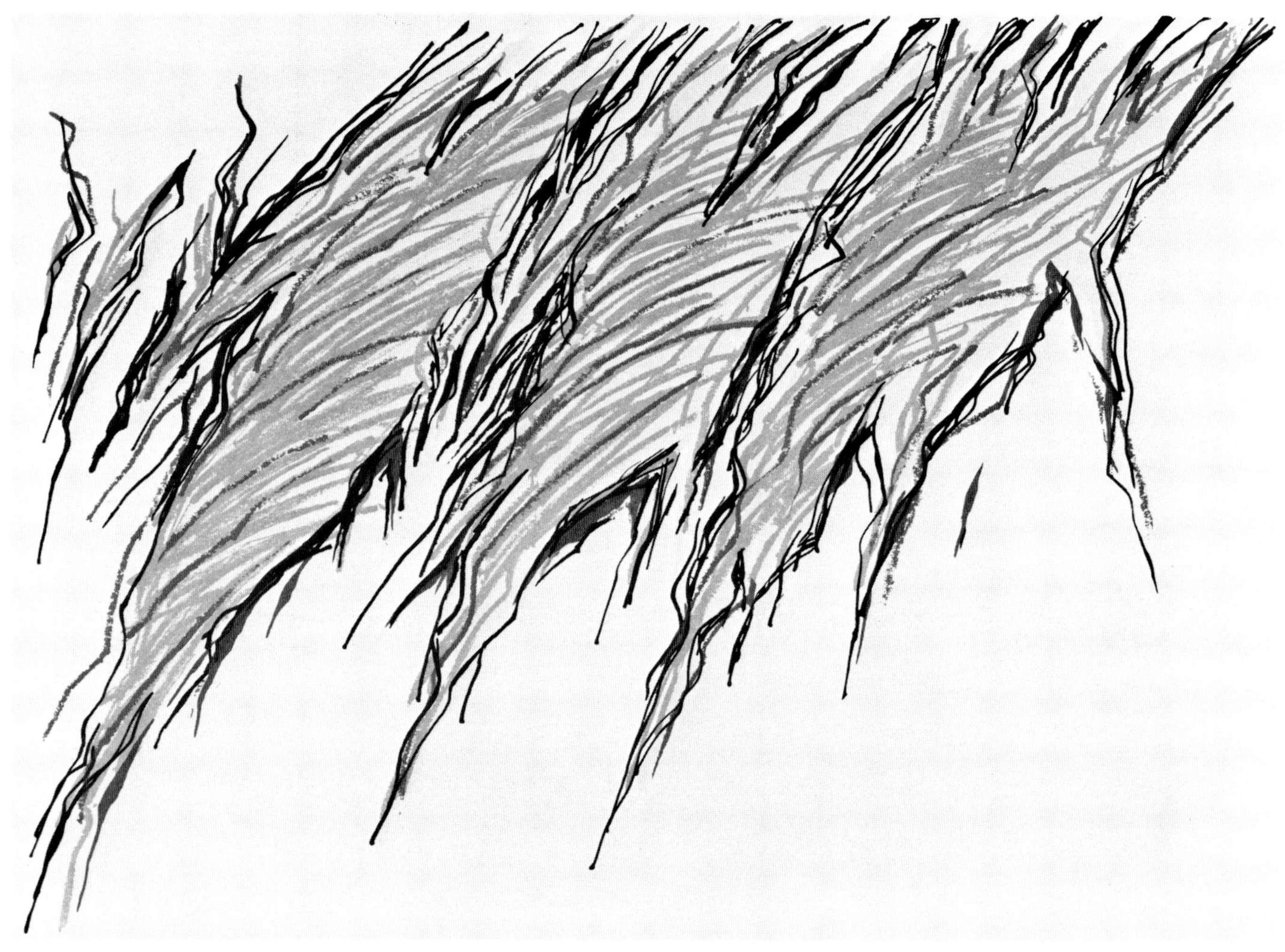

20

**1** *Tarozita*, 1977

*Les oeuvres illustrant le texte apparaissent aux pages 18 et 19.*

*Si Hurtubise a beaucoup appris de l'expressionnisme abstrait
américain, son style s'est developpé en une synthèse et un
amalgame des courants qui ont marqué au Québec la peinture
depuis vingt ans. Car, pour Hurtubise, le geste est une arme
plastique pour inventer des formes nouvelles. Plus qu'une projection autobiographique tributaire de l'expressionnisme, la
peinture d'Hurtubise est aujourd'hui un enchevêtrement de
plans et de lignes donnant lieu à la création d'un espace de
type convexe, s'organisant par juxtaposition d'ondes denses
s'appuyant sur un subtil rayonnement de la couleur. L'am-
biguité des fonds et des surfaces peintes persiste renforçant
"l'effet chavirant" de ces tableaux obliques et désarmants....*

Extraits d'un texte non publié de René Viau

L'art de Jacques Hurtubise et sa personnalité sont, selon la
tradition de l'expressionnisme abstrait intimement unis. Le
peintre transfère ses pulsions, ses instincts, ses angoisses et
ses joies dans le langage des formes et des couleurs. Hurtubise se libère et s'épuise tout à la fois dans sa production.
Son oeuvre est gestuelle, viscérale et violente, choquant plus
qu'elle n'attire, mais elle n'a ni la texture ni l'empâtement caractéristiques à cet art. Gilles Toupin disait de lui:…*"Hurtubise
cherche l'art dans l'actualisation de sa propre existence,…"*[1]
et au début de sa carrière, Hurtubise fit cette remarque au
critique Robert Millet: *"Je peins donc je suis!"*[2] Cependant au
cours des vingt-cinq dernières années, son engagement total
envers la peinture est constamment confirmé par ses déclara-
tions au sujet de son art et de lui-même.

> *Moi, quand je peins, c'est tout, c'est complètement tout,
> tout, tout. Tout ce que je fais. J'ai l'impression que mes
> tableaux, c'est mon miroir, mon image.…Moi puis le
> tableau, c'est juste une affaire. On est poigné ensemble,
> de même…*[3]

> *Si t'aimes pas mes tableaux, c'est moi que t'aimes pas.*[4]

> *Si J'ai Faim, je mange, si j'ai soif, je bois, si je veux voir un
> tableau, je le fais au plus vite…Il y en a qui pensent
> longtemps leurs tableaux avant de les faire.*[5]

> *Moi, j'ai pas le temps de me reculer, r, [sic], de penser à
> …Je pense aux tableaux, en tableaux, puis je fais des
> tableaux.*[6]

> *Je fais mes tableaux un après l'autre, deux et même trois
> à la fois. Quand j'ai fini, c'est parce que je trouve que c'est
> bon, que c'est fort et qu'il m'est impossible de faire
> mieux.*[7]

> *Quand je peins, je suis toujours tendu. Une tension
> épouvantable…Je m'énerve en fumant; je m'énerve en
> marchant;…Mais il faut que je le sois plus pour travailler.
> Autrement, c'est pas possible.*[8]

> *C'est un métier dur tout de même.…Tu mets toute ton
> énergie là-dedans, toute ta vie.*[9]

Tous sont d'accord pour le qualifier d'instinctif, d'impulsif, de
spontané, de généreux et de rigoureux. Il est le reflet de sa
peinture qui traduit des tensions et des pulsions primaires, tout
en utilisant un langage raffiné et ordonné. Le vocabulaire
synthétique d'Hurtubise dérive de l'opposition binaire entre
l'expressionnisme et le formalisme. Déjà en 1966, lors de sa
première new-yorkaise, à la Galerie Marlborough, il se défi-
nissait comme un peintre "à part," et croyait qu'il était possible
d'incorporer un élément personnel dans un art de plus en plus
impersonnel et universel. D'ailleurs, Simone Auger, qui l'inter-
viewait à cette occasion, écrivait:

> *Il conserve une part de fantaisie, se situant dans une
> classe à lui, 'ni purement expressionnisme abstrait, ni
> purement 'Hard Edge'.' Dans un art de plus en plus im-
> personnel et parfois même anonyme, il croit possible
> d'être un peu personnel.*[10]

Dès le début de sa carrière, les critiques l'ont remarqué
grâce à sa détermination, son esprit travailleur et fougueux:
*"Dialecticien, travailleur, nerveux et prolifique: voici Jacques
Hurtubise,…"*[11]
Les tableaux de cette exposition *Jacques Hurtubise:
Oeuvres Récentes* datent de ces trois dernières années et
présentent les importants changements survenus dans la démarche de l'artiste, témoignant ainsi de sa maturité. Ce développement récent ne peut cependant pas être parfaitement
compris sans passer en revue l'oeuvre entière d'Hurtubise.
C'est donc à partir des entrevues accordées par l'artiste et
des articles de critiques d'art comme Simone Auger, Richard
Crevier, Gilles Toupin et Fernande Saint-Martin qui ont vécu le
développement du courant artistique des années soixante et
soixante-dix et suivi la progression de l'oeuvre d'Hurtubise,
que nous présentons les *Oeuvres Récentes*.

### Début de la carrière

*"J'ai fait comme tout le monde."*[12] Hurtubise décrit en ces
quelques mots les tableaux figuratifs exécutés à l'Ecole des
Beaux-Arts de Montréal entre 1956 et 1960. Ces oeuvres
démontrent l'assimilation et l'application des techniques tra-



# JACQUES HURTUBISE:
# OEUVRES RÉCENTES

ditionnelles, le jeu des proportions, de la perspective, des formules de compositions: il peignait alors des paysages et des vues du vieux Port de Montréal, (ill. 1, *Le Port,* 1957). Sa première exposition de groupe eut lieu en 1957, alors qu'il était étudiant aux Beaux-Arts; elle était présentée sur l'Ile Ste-Hélène, au Restaurant Hélène de Champlain, qui servait également de salle d'exposition pour les jeunes artistes. Pierre Saucier parlait ainsi d'Hurtubise et de sa peinture:

> *Jacques Hurtubise est raffiné. Il a un sens aigu de la mobilité. Son paysage de brûlé est d'une délicatesse japonaise. La couleur est ténue, raréfiée comme après la chute des feuilles. Des troncs nus et graciles élèvent leurs baguettes légères sur un ciel bleu-rose-gris, ouaté de douceur et de charme mélancolique.*[13]

A la fin de 1960, il fut boursier de la Fondation Max Beckman et put ainsi séjourner huit mois à New-York où il fit connaissance avec l'art abstrait de Jackson Pollock, Franz Kline, et de Willem de Konning qui influencèrent sa démarche future. Le mouvement accordait une importance primordiale au geste du peintre et à l'expression des sensations immédiates. Hurtubise ne put rester insensible devant ce foisonnement d'idées nouvelles, et affirma que dès ce moment, son oeuvre suivit une nouvelle direction.[14] *Radioactivité No. 4,* 1961 (ill. 2) est le tableau le plus représentatif de cette époque et illustre la primauté du geste libre. Cette composition suggère à la fois le traitement de l'espace considéré comme profondeur et l'ambiguïté résultant de l'ambivalence entre la forme et le fond. Par une recherche dans la manipulation des couleurs et des formes, caractéristiques de l'Expressionnisme abstrait, ses compositions se couvrent de masses non structurées. Mais, mal à l'aise devant ce manque d'organisation inhérent à ce style, il se met à chercher un moyen pour incorporer geste et mouvement dans un format systématique. Sa première solution fut de sectionner l'espace pictural de grosses taches de couleurs qui se juxtaposent, se superposent et parfois se continuent en des traits épais.

Cette recherche conduisit Hurtubise vers les Plasticiens. Ces artistes réunis à Montréal dans les années 50 étaient partisans d'une approche formaliste basée sur des configurations géométriques, la symétrie et les motifs répétitifs; ce mouvement s'opposait à "l'Automatisme," dirigé au Québec par Paul-Emile Borduas. La rigidité formelle soutenue par les Plasticiens répondait au besoin de structure d'Hurtubise. Il opta pour cet élément tout en conversant l'impulsion du geste caractéristique de l'expressionnisme abstrait. Cette synthèse est clairement présentée dans un tableau de 1964, *Quadrature* (ill. 3), et le critique Gilles Toupin disait de cette époque: *"Les notions*

*de géométrisme et de tachisme se confondent pour donner au tableau une entité de dualité, d'ordre et de chaos en un même espace."*[15]

### 1964—Un tournant: la tache et le 'Hard-Edge'

En 1964, Hurtubise adopta un troisième élément dans ses tableaux. En plus de l'impulsion du geste typique à l'expressionnisme abstrait, de l'organisation géométrique et de la répétition des motifs des Plasticiens, il se mit à utiliser des techniques de l'Ecole du Hard-Edge, c'est-à-dire une surface unie avec des arêtes bien découpées. Hurtubise introduisit une forme nouvelle dans ses tableaux la "tache," omniprésente dans ses oeuvres suivantes. En 1966, Richard Crevier, dans son introduction pour la Galerie du Siècle, décrivait la tache comme: *"La spontaneité elle-même, …elle avait la double valeur d'un objet sur un fond et d'un plan sur un espace."*[16] Même si la forme apparaissait comme éclatée sur un fond uni, un examen plus attentif révèle un motif dépouillé de tout attribut, réduit à une forme intrinsèque et anonyme, intégré dans son style géométrique. La tache est devenue élément-forme répété et inversé sur des axes géométriques atténuant la différence entre le fond et la forme. Fernande Saint-Martin écrivait ceci à propos des tableaux de 1966 dans *Art International:*

> *Il procède à un travail d'élaboration plus ou moins mécanique du contour de la tache pour lui enlever son expressivité et son lyrisme, pour montrer qu'une tache est aussi "non expressive" qu'un élément formel régulier.… que c'est autant le plan vertical qui constitue l'élément-tache que la tache qui devient plan;…*[17]

Le choix de couleurs pures et vibrantes a augmenté la tension créée par l'élimination de la forme et du fond. Ce procédé est devenu encore plus évident dans certains tableaux comme *Iris,* peint en 1966, (ill. 4). Dans cette oeuvre la tache devient une série de formes libres reproduites avec un pochoir, équilibrant le fond et la forme dans le cadre d'une structure géométrique, provoquant ainsi un jeu de réversibilité du motif et du fond. Même si en apparence elles sont très proches du mouvement OP, ces formes étaient déjà présentes dans des tableaux antérieurs et reflétaient la persévérance d'Hurtubise dans sa recherche de structure ordonnée. Il modifia aussi la position de la toile, avec ses plans horizontaux et verticaux interchangeables pour une orientation en diagonale. Cette préoccupation d'éliminer la définition de l'espace positif et négatif et les effets optiques produits par l'application de couleurs contrastantes et vibrantes, annonçait l'exploration dans le domaine de la luminosité, qu'Hurtubise entreprendra au cours de l'année suivante.

## 1967—Les néons

En 1967, Hurtubise fut invité comme artiste en résidence au Collège de Dartmouth, à Hanover dans le New Hampshire, où il prépara les tableaux qui représentèrent le Canada à la IX Biennale de São Paulo au Brésil. A cette époque sa recherche dans le domaine de la luminosité s'intensifiait et l'ammena à exécuter des "tableaux-lumière." Dans une entrevue accordée à Fernande Saint-Martin lors de sa rétrospective au Musée d'art contemporain en 1973, Hurtubise définit ainsi sa démarche: *"Avant les oeuvres au néon, dans ma recherche de lumière, j'avais fait des tableaux si lumineux qu'ils étaient presque blancs. Et je n'ai pu que passer ensuite aux néons."*[18]

Pour échapper aux limitations imposées par l'opacité résiduelle inhérente aux matières pigmentées des médiums, il commença à manipuler le spectre des couleurs optiques des néons afin d'obtenir un maximum de luminosité. Hurtubise répondit en ces mots à Normand Thériault qui l'interrogeait au sujet de cette nouvelle attitude *"…Si j'ai fait des néons, c'est parce que je ne pouvais pas avoir de la peinture électrique en pot! …Mes néons ne sont pas pour moi des sculptures; ce sont des tableaux."*[19] Cette remarque indiquait qu'il cherchait, à transposer une expression plastique d'un medium à un autre et qu'il n'avait pas l'intention de tirer parti des rythmes sculpturaux, associés à l'art des néons pendant les années soixante. *Ciboulette,* 1969 (ill. 5) témoigne de cette époque et démontre qu'une transformation radicale d'un médium n'aboutit pas à la création d'un nouvel univers formel. Bien que son objectif d'approfondir sa recherche sur la luminosité semblait avoir été accompli par l'utilisation des néons, Hurtubise dut abandonner ses tableaux-lumière et retourna aux techniques traditionnelles pour des raisons d'ordre financier et d'énergie personnelle.

## 1970—Les carrés égaux

A partir des années soixante-dix, le carré, un élément familier souvent dissimulé par la couleur et par le jeu de réversibilité entre la forme et le fond, devenait un facteur important dans la composition de ces tableaux. Et au cours des années suivantes, le carré constituera la structure principale et la force majeure de son style. Dans un tableau du début de cette période, *Marie-Jeanne,* 1970 (ill. 6) des motifs diagonaux en zigzag s'opposent à une structure quadrillée semblable à des taches géométriques. Les verts-acides, les roses et les oranges fluorescents s'alignent sur un fond noir dans un contraste maximal et révèlent l'exploration des possibilités optiques de la couleur. Le découpage du motif permet une lecture diagonale tout en obstruant la distinction entre la forme et le fond.

Peu à peu le noir se mit à envahir le tableau et ce n'était qu'à la périphérie de la grille que des soubresauts de couleurs fluorescentes apparaissaient. Ainsi les couleurs accentuaient le quadrillé et produisaient des effets lumineux.

En 1972, au lieu de peindre une grille sur la toile, Hurtubise a décidé de fractionner le support du tableau en carrés égaux, amovibles qui devinrent des éléments autonomes arrangés au gré de l'artiste pour créer un ensemble (super-structure). Une fois agencés, les carrés perdirent leur qualité d'éléments autonomes et devinrent une construction permanente et cohérente. Hurtubise expliquait ce changement lors d'une entrevue avec Saint-Martin:

> *J'en avais assez des structures en grille, des modules, des recherches chromatiques subtiles. J'ai complétement transformé ma façon de travailler, de produire 'le tableau.'*[20]

Hurtubise s'est détaché de la grille qui limitait sa composition. Bien qu'il peignait toujours sur le même format, le carré, il s'est dégagé de l'immédiate nécessité d'organiser et de composer l'ensemble du tableau. Une fois peints, les éléments amovibles permettaient une infinité de combinaisons et d'arrangements avant la composition finale. Gilles Toupin dans un article pour le quotidien *La Presse* comparait ce style à un jeu: *"…l'idée de ludisme existe dans cette construction qui instaure l'art au niveau du jeu, mais un jeu profondément ancré dans un projet fondamental d'existence: celui d'être peintre."*[21]

Les oeuvres des années suivantes restèrent fidèles à l'utilisation du procédé à carreaux amovibles, la couleur n'était plus traitée comme l'élément dynamique principal; les formes, les contours, les dégoulinades et les taches appliqués avec soin s'orientaient de plus en plus vers l'oblique de la toile, créant un mouvement et une énergie internes qui semblaient se projeter hors du tableau. Des couleurs contrastantes comme des noirs et des rouges, des roses et des jaunes se juxtaposent, se superposent pour amplifier le jeu des formes et du fond sans toutefois définir l'espace positif et négatif. *Roxie,* peint en 1974 (ill. 7) représente cette phase. Dans cette peinture complexe tout est ordonné, rien n'est laissé au hasard, bien que le geste semble libre et impulsif. Hurtubise lui-même affirme souvent que plus ses tableaux ont l'air spontané, plus ils sont en réalité construits. Il élimine tout risque d'accident dans ses oeuvres en apparence gestuelles et sans retenue, en masquant même les bords les plus irréguliers et les plus inorganiques.

## 1977–1980: Nouvelle orientation

En 1977, les peintures-modulaires dominent l'oeuvre d'Hurtubise avec des tableaux comme *Tapéribonka* (cat. no. 2) et

*Tatacouna* (cat. no. 3), les premiers en date de l'exposition. L'organisation des carrés aboutit à une synthèse des travaux antérieurs et constitue également le point de départ d'une recherche qu'Hurtubise poursuivra au cours des deux prochaines années. Dans *Tatacouna,* trois taches occupent le centre de la toile comme des formes éclatées et aplaties sur un fond: des traits linéaires et gestuels rayonnent des taches. Ces traits deviendront l'élément crucial du développement futur de sa peinture. Dans deux oeuvres suivantes, *Tawakiki,* (cat. no. 4) et *Texite,* (cat. no. 5), peintes en 1978, Hurtubise reprend le langage spontané et gestuel qu'il utilisait dans ses premiers tableaux comme *Impatience,* 1961 (ill. 8). Ces tableaux ne représentent plus des formes planes occupant des espaces ambigus mais décrivent des volumes curvilignes et pour la première fois ils introduisent la notion de perspective et de distance. Hurtubise abandonne le module ou la grille comme élément de composition dans ces oeuvres récentes et chaque peinture devient la description d'une masse topologique unique.

En 1978, le sujet des oeuvres dans *Taniwaki* (cat. no. 6) et *Tawapitie* (cat. no. 7) se raffine et se simplifie; les formes sobres aux arêtes définies suggèrent de vastes étendues gonflées et des esquisses de masses ressemblant à des paysages. Les formes et le contraste de la couleur sur un fond neutre décrivent des motifs linéaires et créent un jeu de tensions tel que la surface même de la toile semble étirée et bombée. L'observation des tableaux choisis pour cette exposition révèlent la continuation de représentation de paysages et de volumes globaux.

Les oeuvres selectionnées de 1979, *Takarakas,* (cat. no. 8) *Tadoussac,* (cat. no. 9) *Tafarina,* (cat. no. 10) *Taflanelle,* (cat. no. 12) et *Tamarakas* (cat. no. 13) sont caractérisées par des formes ressemblant à des traits courts et abrégés qui décrivent des masses mouvantes. Ces tableaux conservent encore leurs surfaces lisses typiques du travail d'Hurtubise depuis 1964, mais ils indiquent une progression de son style. Dans les tableaux de 1980, *Texado* (cat. no. 14) et *Tazuni* (cat. no. 15), on remarque que la texture de la surface accentue les qualités gestuelles et curvilignes de son style grâce à des couches de peinture plus épaisses, et que l'application de pastel ou de fusain ajoute une note de couleur et définit le volume. La peinture d'Hurtubise a subi des changements stylistiques et techniques et ainsi elle a évolué, mais le trait essentiel qui émerge de l'ensemble de son oeuvre est la constance.

Des allusions aux scènes du vieux port de Montréal qu'il peignait auparavant transparaissent tout au long de son oeuvre. Avec ces travaux récents, moins plats et unidimensionnels il crée l'illusion d'un rendu topographique, l'artiste revient à son point de départ et se remet à faire une peinture qui, même si elle manque de "spécificité" organique, reste néanmoins une description de paysage dans sa forme la plus abstraite.

**Mary-Venner Shee**

[1] Gilles Toupin, "Ces tableaux à noms de femmes," *La Presse* (Montreal), 10 février 1973, sec. D, p. 14.

[2] Robert Millet, "Jacques Hurtubise: Je peins donc je suis!" *Le Magazine Maclean* (Montreal), février 1969, p. 55.

[3] Pierre Pelletier, "Jacques Hurtubise, peintre," *Le Droit* (Ottawa), 30 avril 1977, p. 18.

[4] Gilles Toupin, "Hurtubise et les transes de l'Amérique," *La Presse* (Montreal), 26 octobre 1974, sec. E, p. 19.

[5] Millet, "Jacques Hurtubise: Je peins donc je suis!" p. 55.

[6] Pelletier, "Jacques Hurtubise, peintre," p. 18.

[7] Toupin, "Hurtubise et les transes de l'Amérique," p. 19.

[8] Pelletier, "Jacques Hurtubise, peintre," p. 18.

[9] Toupin, "Hurtubise et les transes de l'Amérique," p. 19.

[10] Simone Auger, "Hurtubise: Quand on a réussi à Montréal, on n'est pas rendu bien loin," *La Presse* (Montreal), 16 juillet 1966, p. 13.

[11] Robert Millet, "Hurtubise vers l'abstraction," *Le Magazine Maclean* (Montreal), février 1962, p. 53.

[12] Auger, "Hurtubise: Quand on a réussi à Montréal…," p. 13.

[13] Pierre Saucier, "Les promesses artistiques de demain à Hélène de Champlain," *La Patrie* (Montreal), 24 novembre 1957, p. 130.

[14] Auger, "Hurtubise: Quand on a réussi à Montréal…," p. 13.

[15] Toupin, "Ces tableaux à noms de femmes," p. 14.

[16] Richard Crevier, *Jacques Hurtubise.* (Montreal: Galerie du Siècle Inc., 1966), n. pag.

[17] Fernande Saint-Martin, "Lettre de Montréal, Jacques Hurtubise," *Art International,* février 1966, p. 47.

[18] Saint-Martin, "Jacques Hurtubise," *Atelier* (Montreal), février 1973, pp. 1–2.

[19] Normand Thériault, "Hurtubise 'je suis instinctif,'" *La Presse* (Montreal), 25 octobre 1969, p. 39.

[20] Saint-Martin, "Jacques Hurtubise," pp. 1–2.

[21] Toupin, "Hurtubise et les transes de l'Amérique," p. 19.

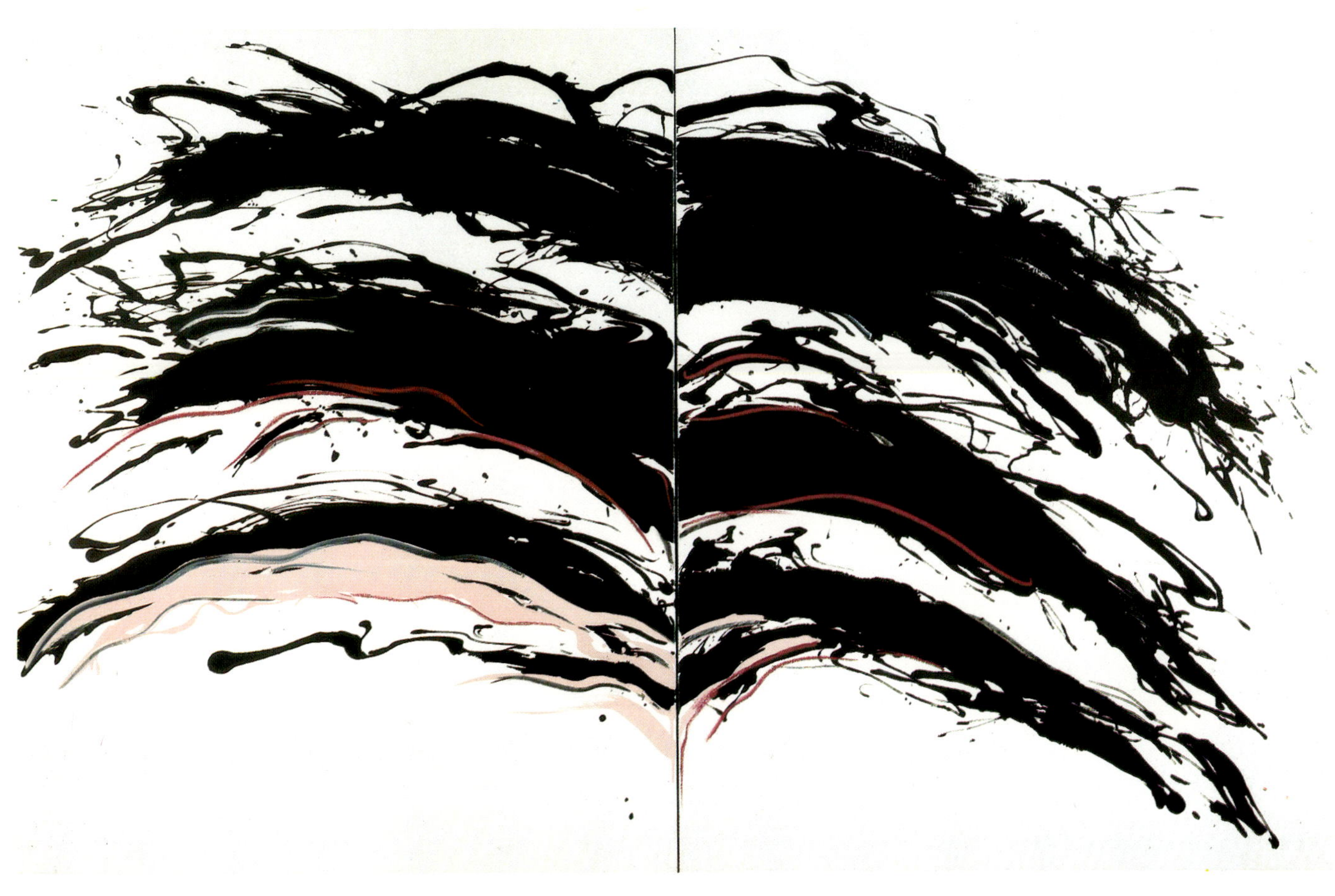



15 *Tazuni,* 1980

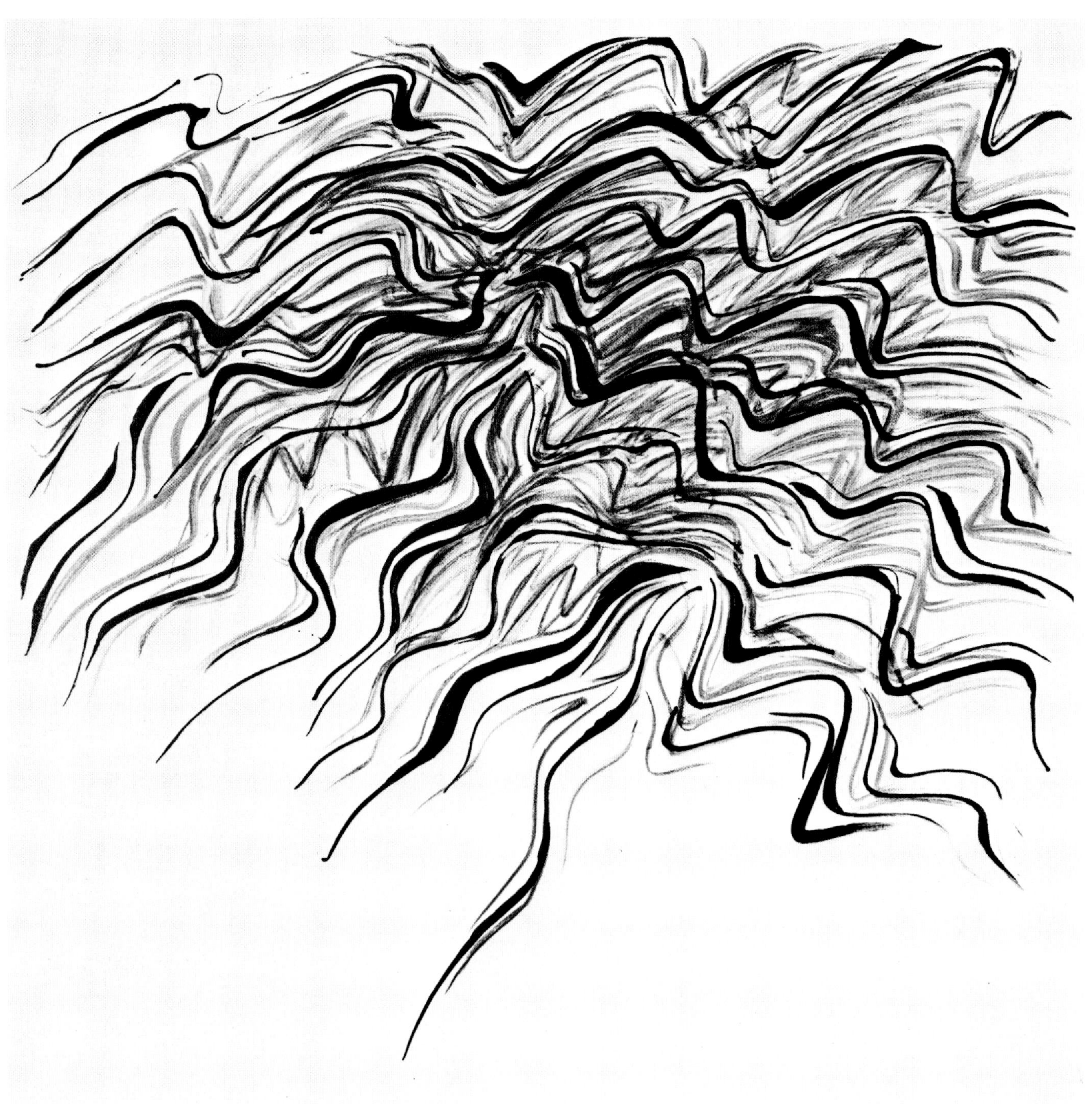

26

**8** *Takarakas*, 1979

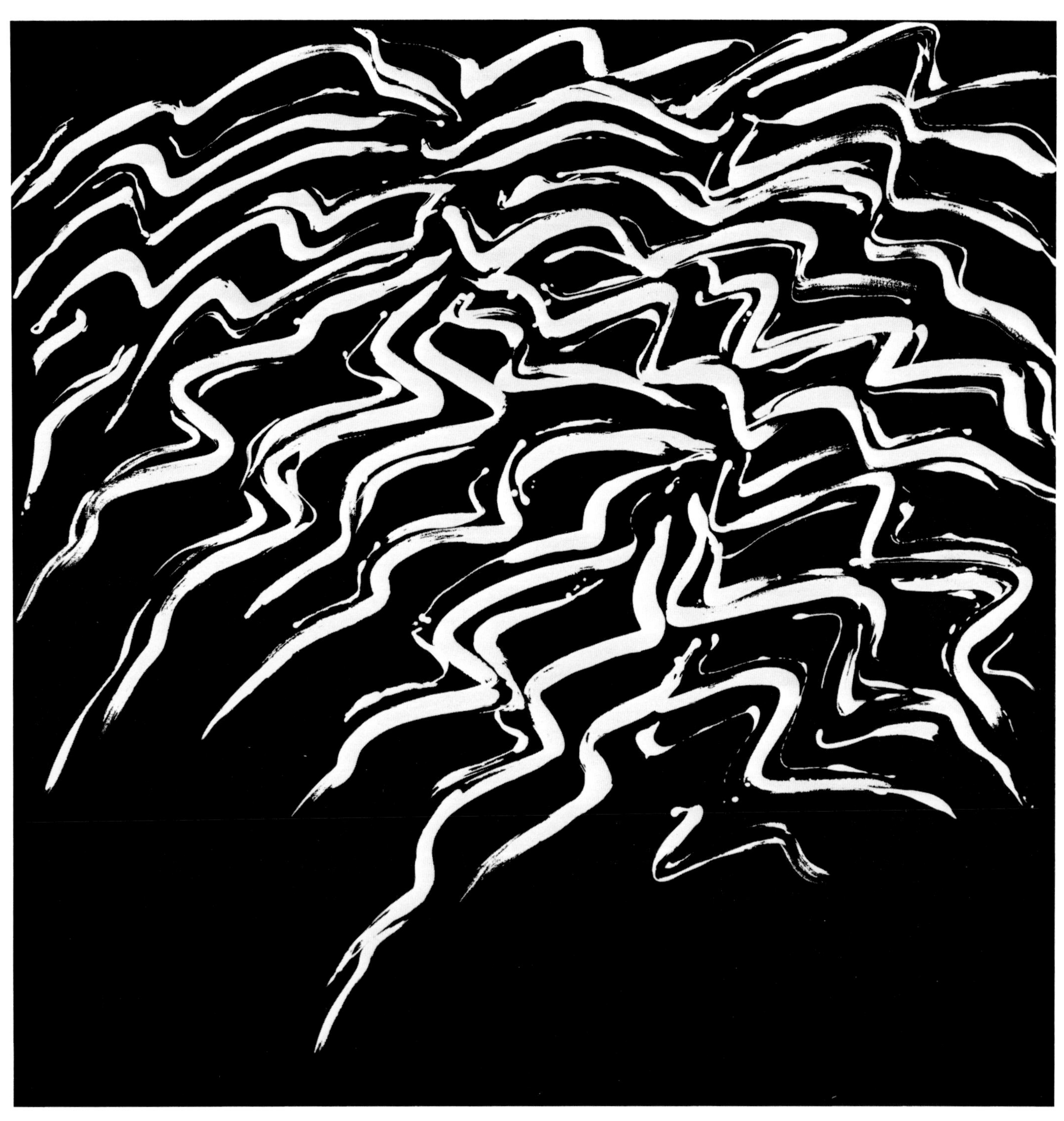

**9** *Tadoussac,* 1979

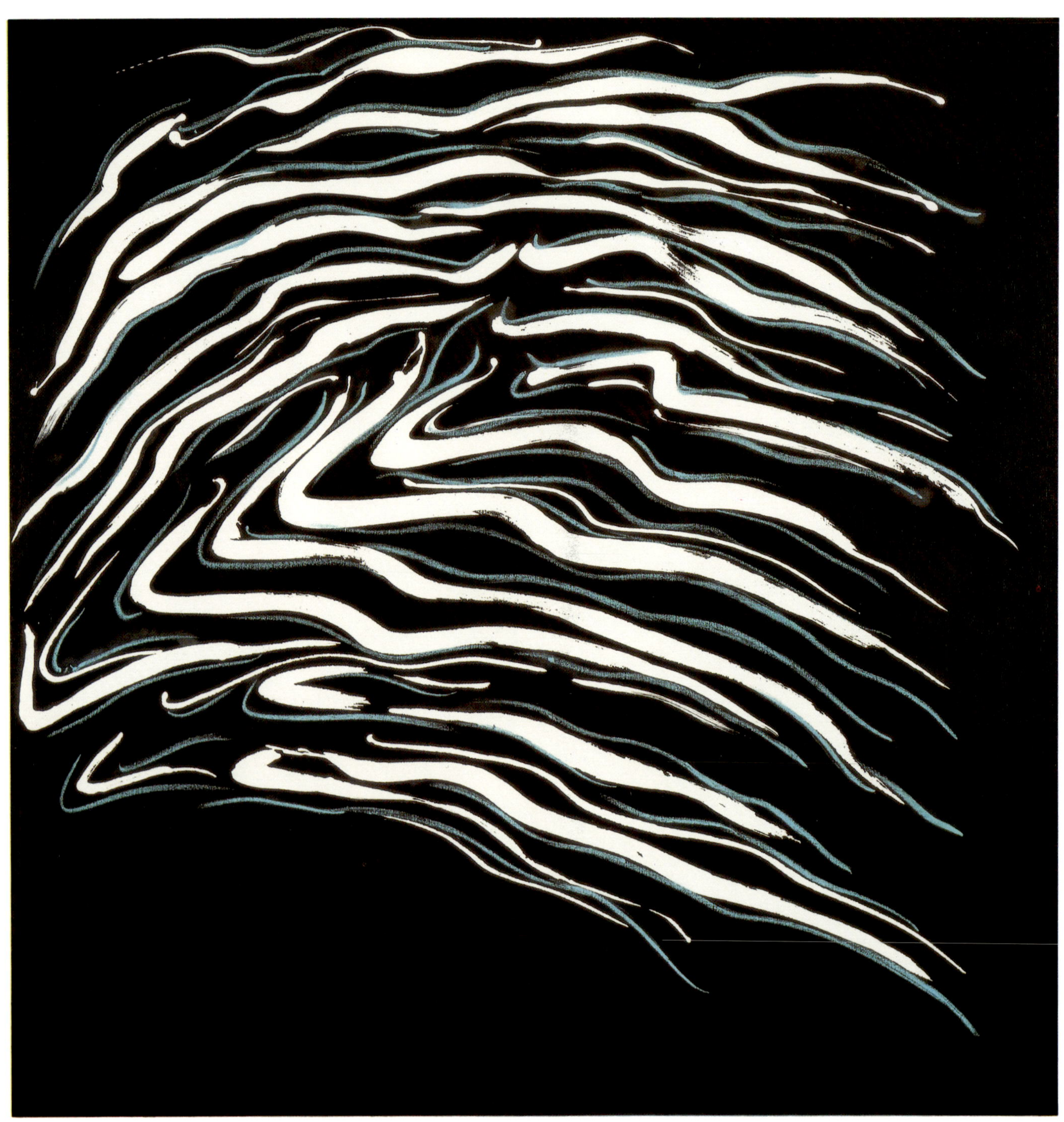

28

**13** *Tamarakas, 1979*

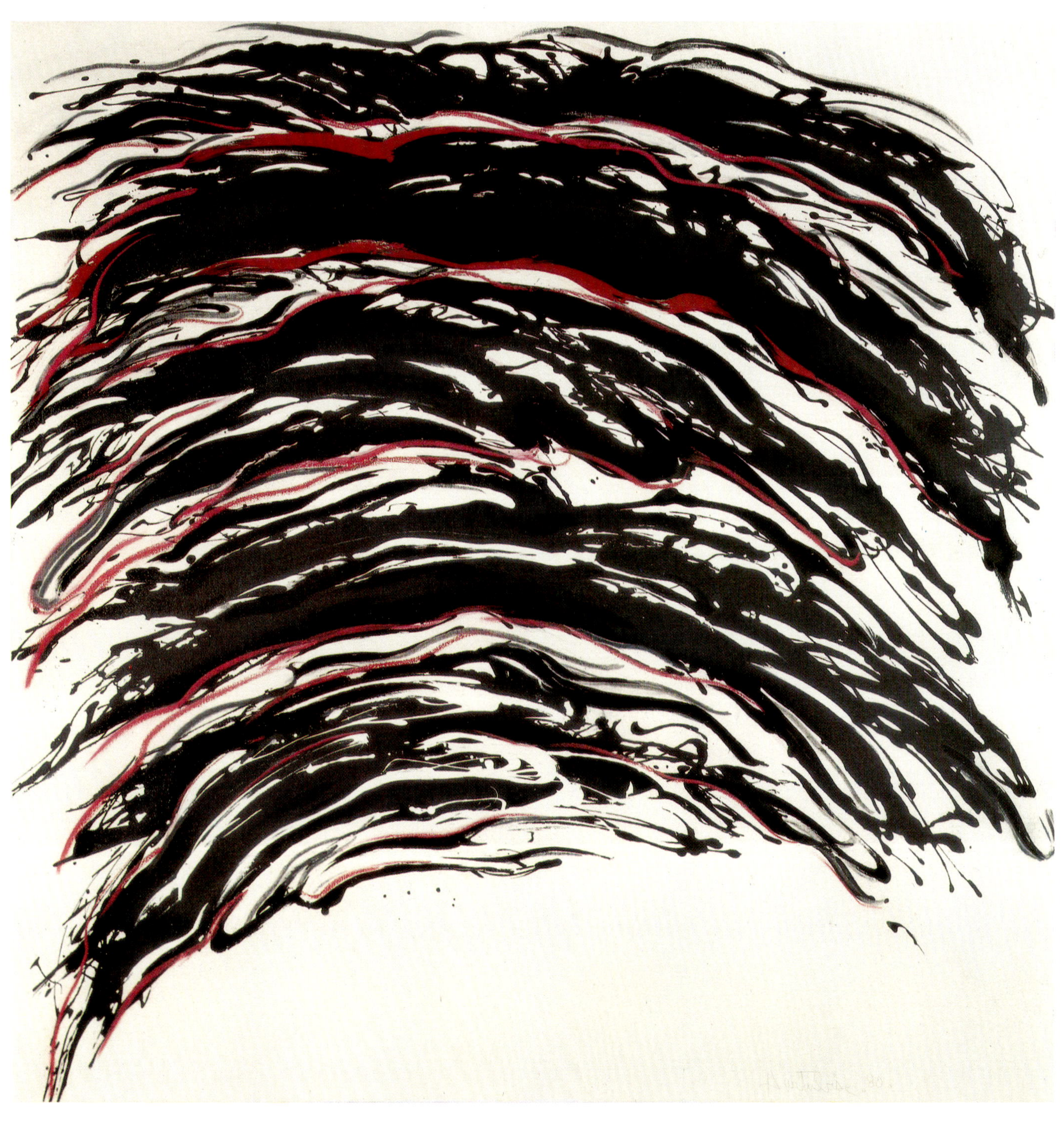



**14** *Texado*, 1980

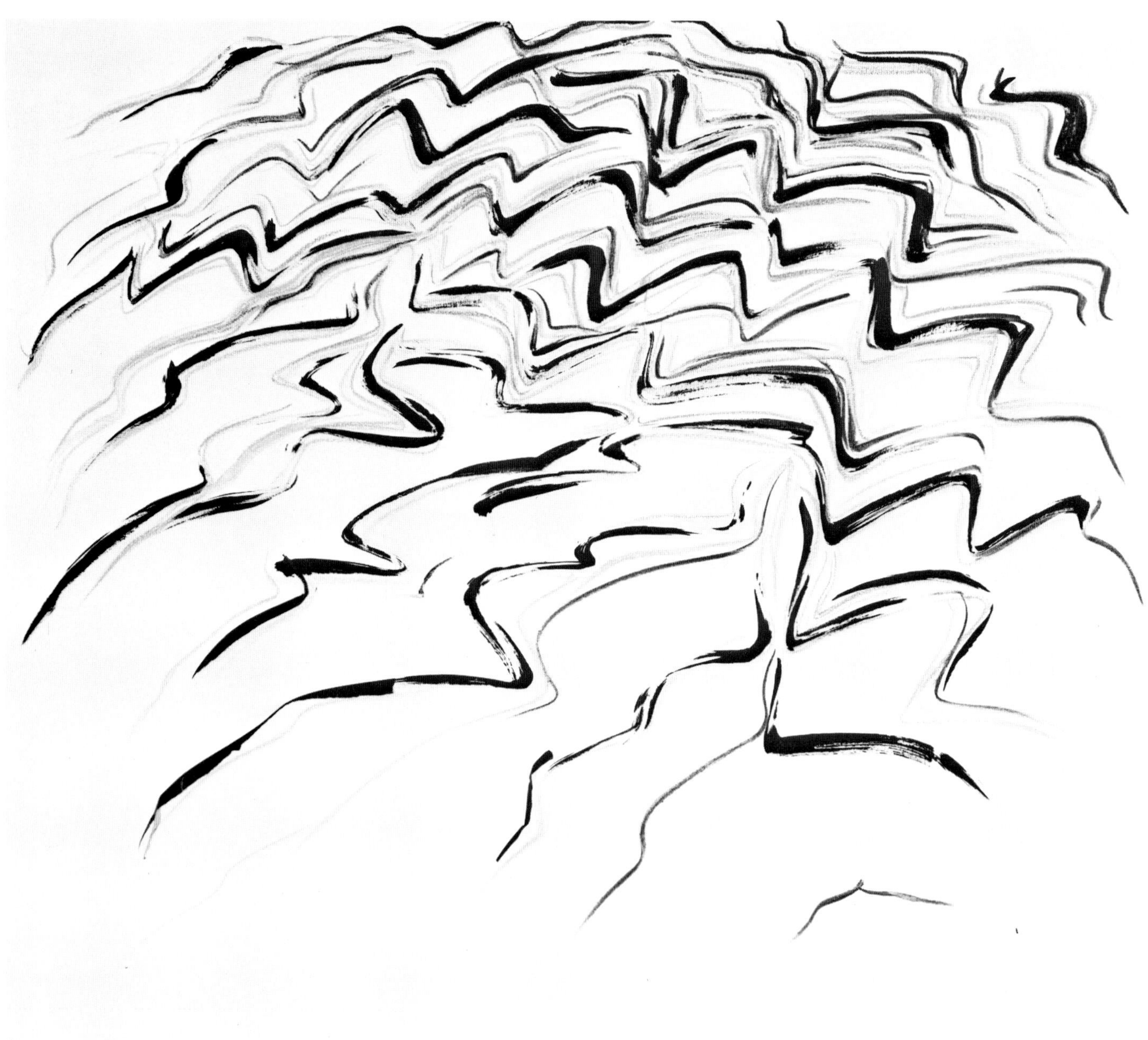



**10** *Tafarina,* 1979

1  *Tarozita*, 1977
Serigraph/Sérigraphie, 42/150
11 x 16 (28 x 40.7)

2  *Tapéribonka*, 1977
Acrylic and charcoal on canvas/Acrylique et fusain sur toile
48 x 64 (121.9 x 162.6)

3  *Tatacouna*, 1977
Acrylic and charcoal on canvas/Acrylique et fusain sur toile
48 x 80 (121.9 x 203.2)

4  *Tawakiki*, 1978
Acrylic, charcoal and pastel on canvas/Acrylique, fusain et
pastel sur toile
48 x 48 (121.9 x 121.9)

5  *Texite*, 1978
Acrylic, charcoal and pastel on canvas/Acrylique, fusain et
pastel sur toile
48 x 64 (121.9 x 162.6)

6  *Taniwaki*, 1978
Acrylic, charcoal and pastel on canvas/Acrylique, fusain et
pastel sur toile
29 x 29 (73.7 x 73.7)

7  *Tawapitie*, 1978
Acrylic, charcoal and pastel on canvas/Acrylique, fusain et
pastel sur toile
29 x 29 (73.7 x 73.7)

8  *Takarakas*, 1979
Acrylic and charcoal on canvas/Acrylique et fusain sur toile
60 x 60 (152.4 x 152.4)

9  *Tadoussac*, 1979
Acrylic on canvas/Acrylique sur toile
60 x 60 (152.4 x 152.4)

10  *Tafarina*, 1979
Acrylic, charcoal and pastel on canvas/Acrylique, fusain et
pastel sur toile
60 x 60 (152.4 x 152.4)

11  *Tavanille*, 1979
Serigraph/Sérigraphie 12/25
22¼ x 22¼ (56.5 x 56.5)

12  *Taflanelle*, 1979
Acrylic and charcoal on canvas/Acrylique et fusain sur toile
60 x 45 (152.4 x 114.3)

13  *Tamarakas*, 1979
Acrylic and pastel on canvas/Acrylique et pastel sur toile
60 x 60 (152.4 x 152.4)

14  *Texado*, 1980
Acrylic, charcoal and pastel on canvas/Acrylique, fusain et
pastel sur toile
60 x 60 (152.4 x 152.4)

15  *Tazuni*, 1980
Acrylic, charcoal and pastel on canvas/Acrylique, fusain et
pastel sur toile
60 x 60 (152.4 x 152.4)

16  *Long Beach*, 1980
Serigraph/Sérigraphie, 4/40
21 x 36 (50.4 x 86.4)



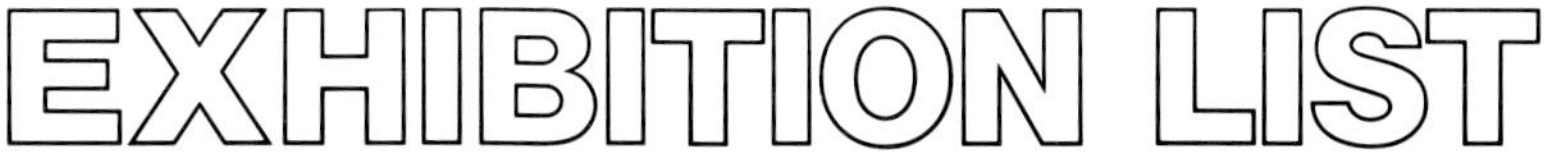

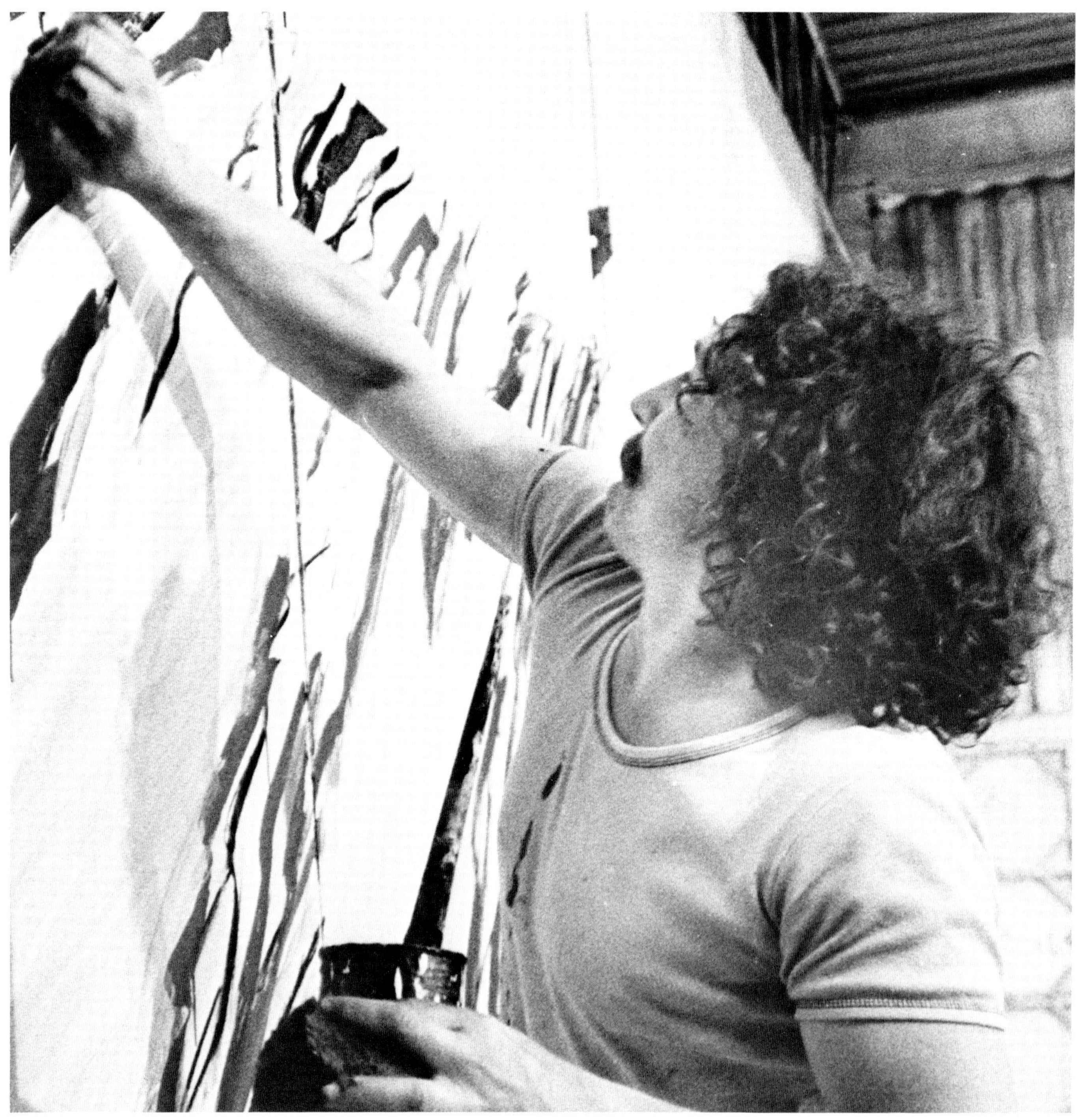

Jacques Hurtubise, 1980

All dimensions are given in inches and centimeters, height preceding width; unless otherwise noted, all works courtesy of the artist. Toutes dimensions sont données en pouces et en centimètres la hauteur précédant la largeur. Sauf indication contraire, toutes les oeuvres sont la courtoisie de l'artiste.

# SELECTED WORKS

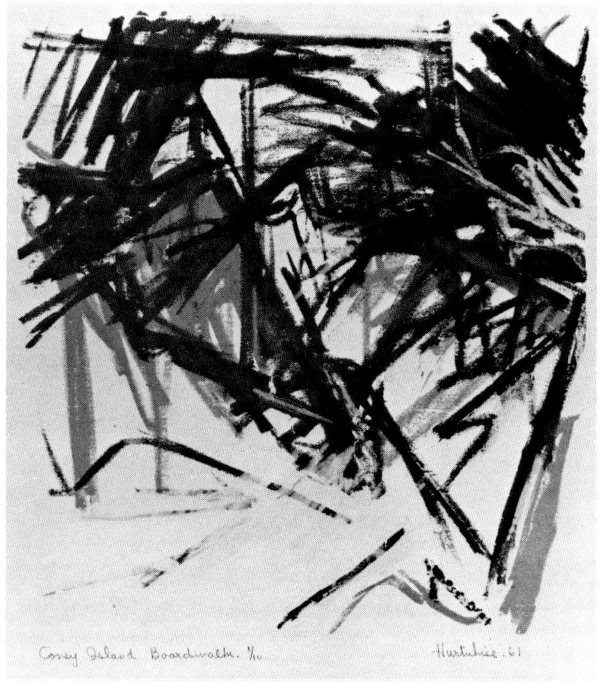

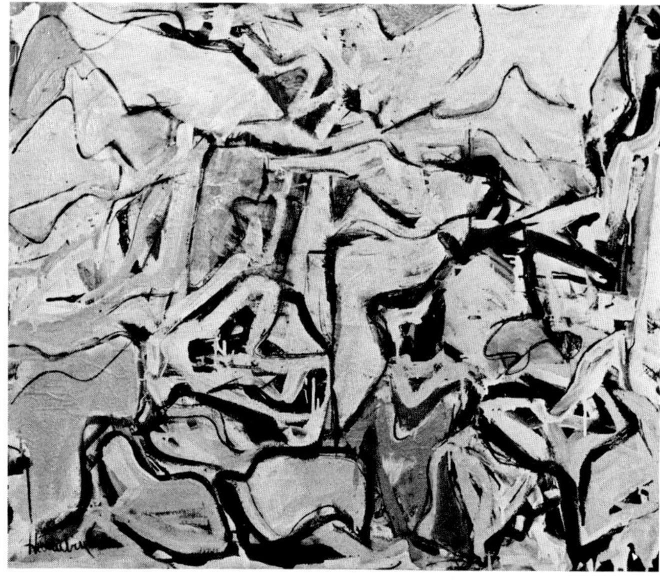

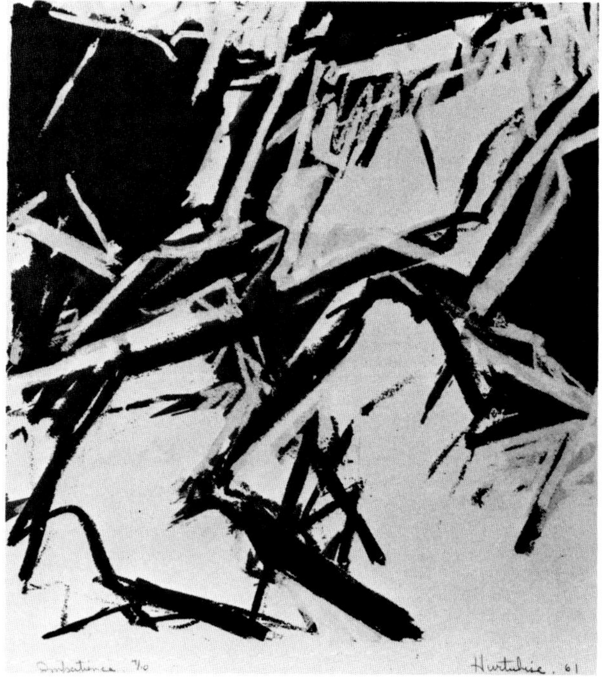

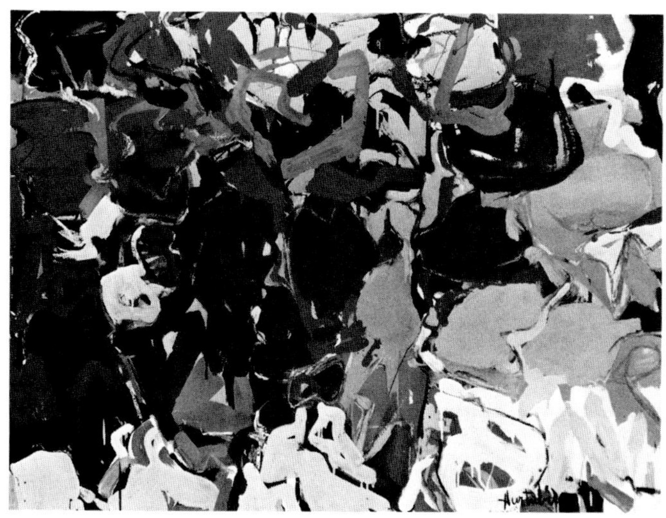



**1** *Coney Island Boardwalk,* 1961
Serigraph/Sérigraphie 1/10
18½ x 17 (47 x 43.2)

**2** *Impatience,* 1961
Serigraph/Sérigraphie 7/10
18½ x 17 (47 x 43.2)

**3** *Radioactivité No. 1,* 1961
Enamel and charcoal on canvas/Email et fusain sur toile
36 x 41 (91.5 x 104.2)

**4** *Radioactivité No. 4,* 1961
Enamel, charcoal and pastel on Masonite/Email, fusain et
pastel sur Masonite
36 x 48 (91.4 x 121.9)

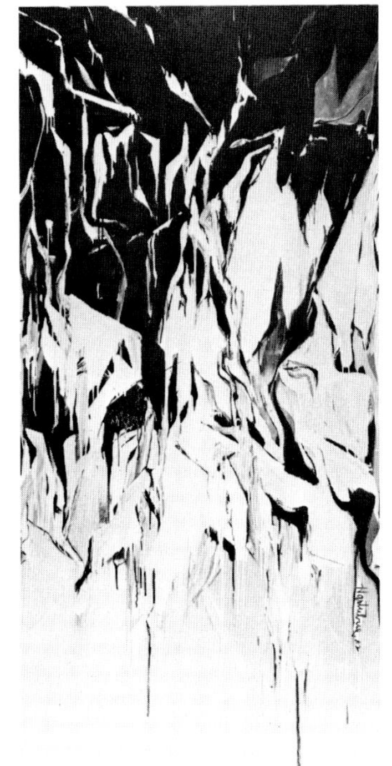
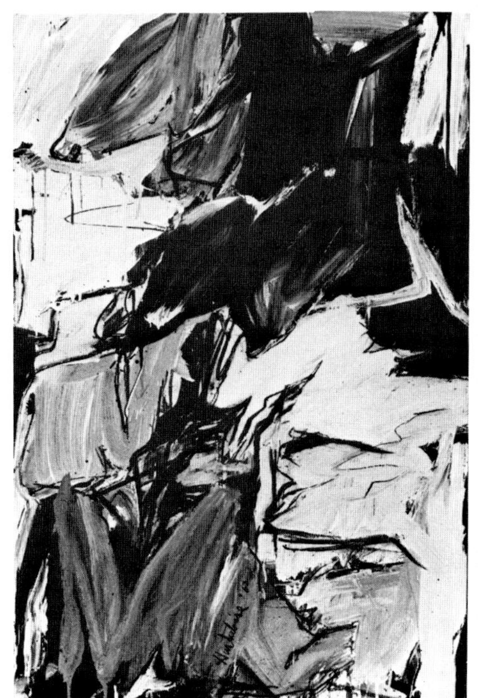
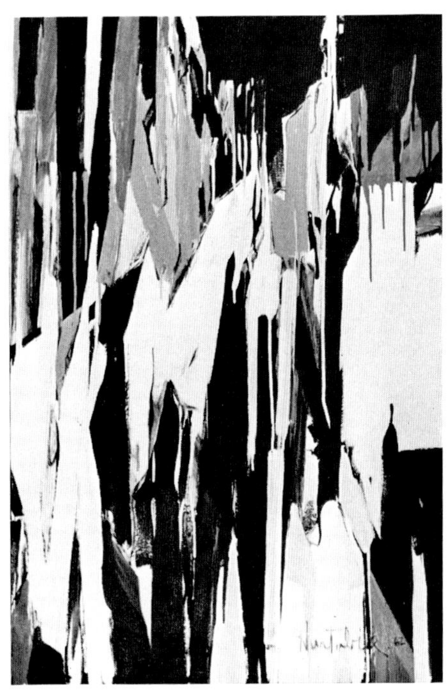
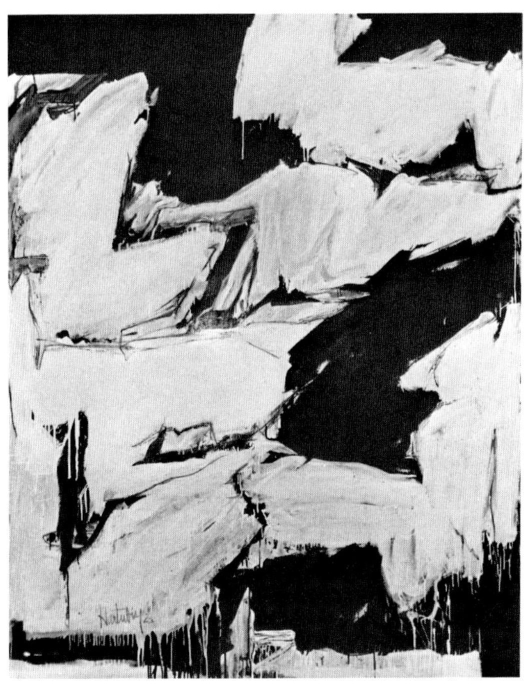

**5** *Peinture No. 5,* 1962
Enamel and charcoal on Masonite/Email et fusain sur Masonite
96 x 48 (243.8 x 121.9)

**6** *Peinture No. 10,* 1962
Enamel on Masonite/Email sur Masonite
48 x 32 (121.9 x 81.3)

**7** *Peinture No. 36,* 1962
Enamel and charcoal on Masonite/Email et fusain sur Masonite
48 x 32 (121.9 x 81.3)

**8** *Peinture No. 44,* 1963
Acrylic and charcoal on canvas/Acrylique et fusain sur toile
83 x 66 (210.8 x 167.6)
Collection of The Canada Council Art Bank/Collection de la
Banque d'oeuvres d'art, du Conseil des Arts du Canada,
Ottawa

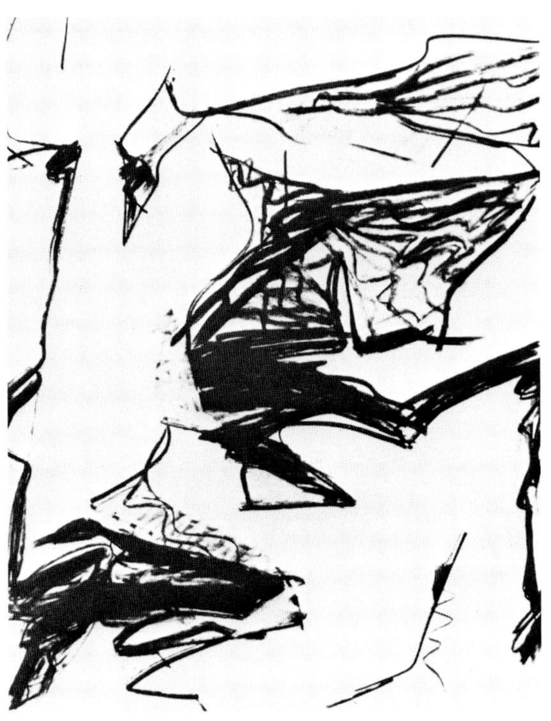

**9** *Numéro Soixante-Dix-Sept,* 1963
Charcoal on paper/Fusain sur papier
25 x 20 (63.5 x 50.8)
Collection of The Sir George Williams University, Montreal

**10** *Perpétuel Isolement,* 1964
Acrylic on canvas/Acrylique sur toile
70 x 50 (177.8 x 127)

**11** *Agonie,* 1964
Acrylic on canvas/Acrylique sur toile
70 x 50 (177.8 x 127)
Collection of Patrick and Andrée Drouin, Quebec

**12** *Quadrature,* 1964
Acrylic on paper/Acrylique sur papier
24 x 20 (61 x 50.8)
Collection of Monique Colangelo, Terrebonne

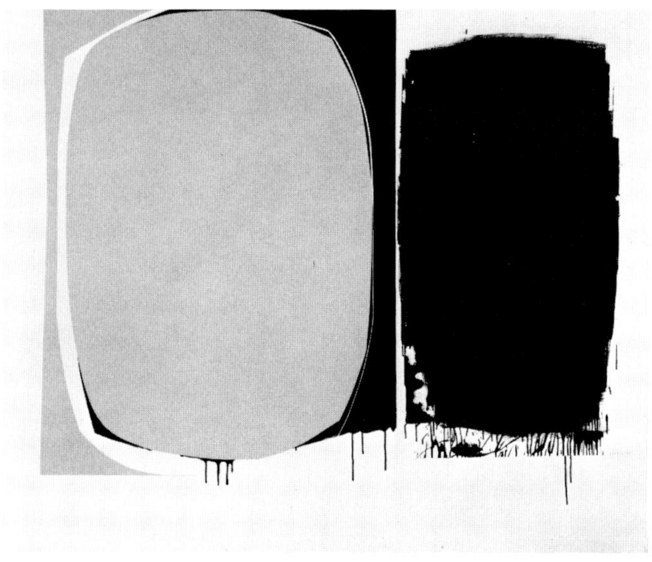

**13** *Aventurine*, 1965
Acrylic on canvas/Acrylique sur toile
48 x 60 (121.9 x 152.4)

**14** *Clara*, 1965
Acrylic on canvas/Acrylique sur toile
60 x 72 (152.3 x 182.9)

**15** *Florence*, 1965
Acrylic on canvas/Acrylique sur toile
48 x 48 (121.9 x 121.9)
Private collection, Montreal

**16** *Katia*, 1965
Acrylic on canvas/Acrylique sur toile
66 x 120 (167.6 x 304.8)
Collection of The National Gallery of Canada/Galerie nationale
du Canada, Ottawa

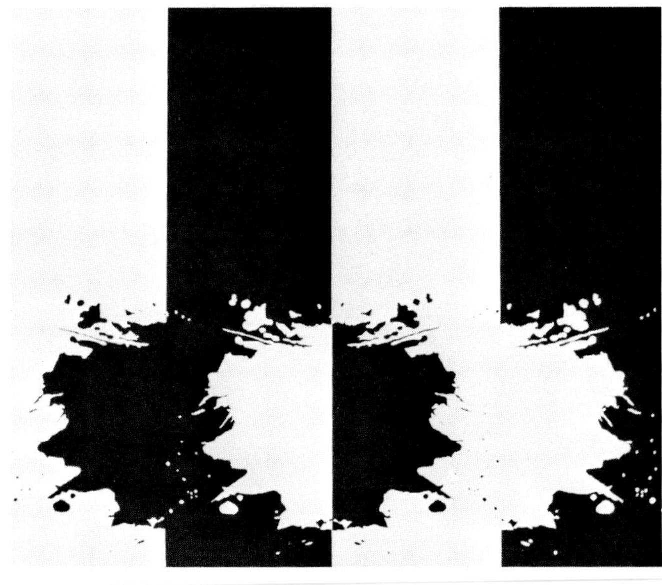
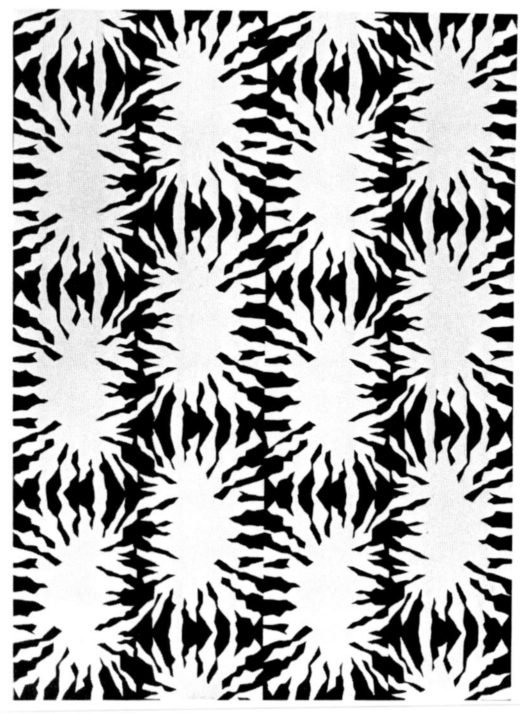
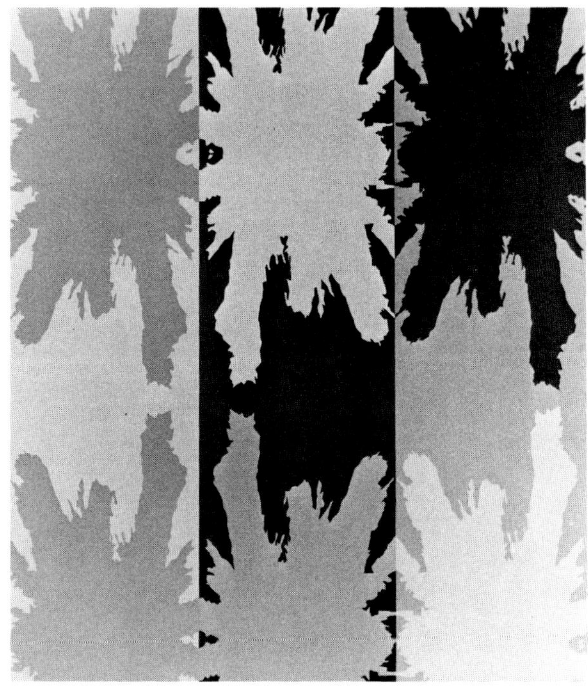
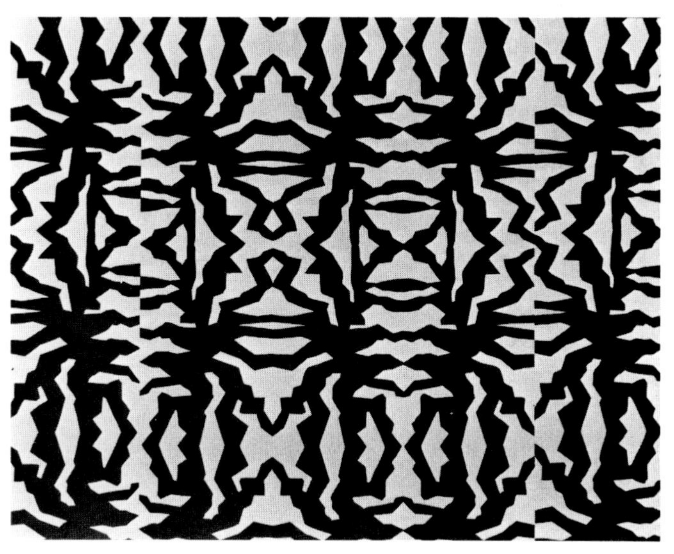



**17** *Karina*, 1965
Acrylic on canvas/Acrylique sur toile
51 x 57 (129.5 x 144.8)
Collection of Bernard Lamarre, Montreal

**18** *Sara*, 1966
Acrylic on canvas/Acrylique sur toile
57 x 51 (144.8 x 129.5)
Collection of Patrick and Andrée Drouin, Quebec

**19** *Yolande*, 1966
Acrylic on canvas/Acrylique sur toile
52 x 46 (132.1 x 116.8)
Collection of Jean Avon, Montreal

**20** *Sans Titre*, 1966
Acrylic on canvas/Acrylique sur toile
46 x 60 (116.8 x 152.4)

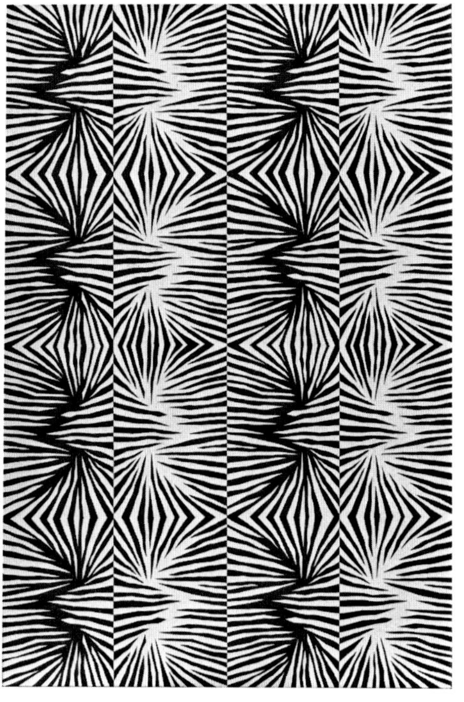

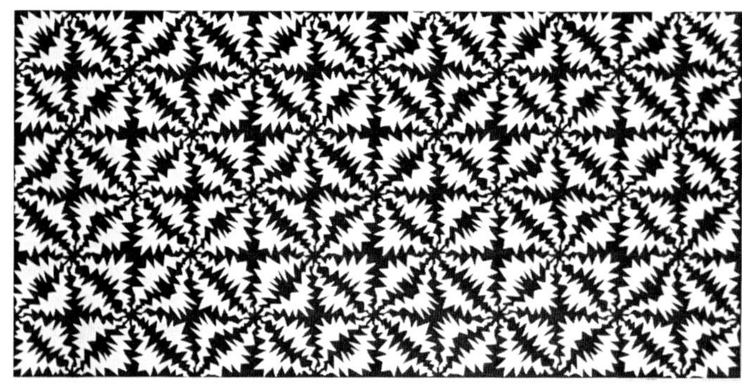

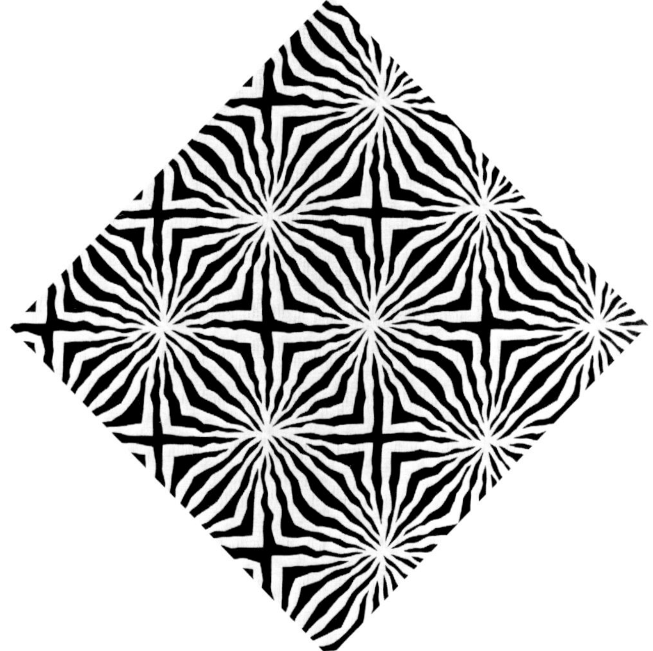

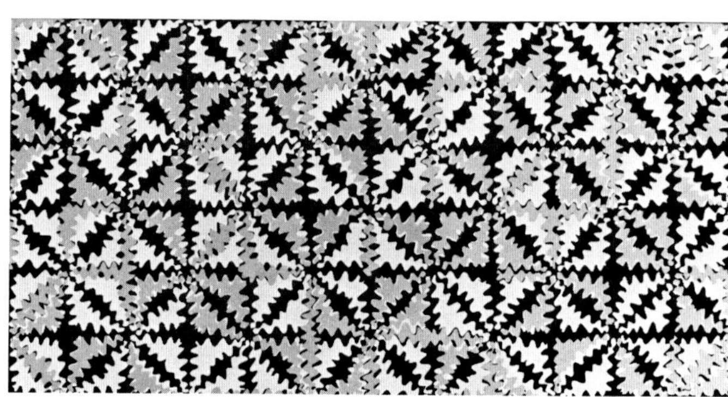



**21** *Diane*, 1966
Acrylic on canvas/Acrylique sur toile
96 x 66 (243.7 x 167.6)
Collection of the Massachussetts Institute of Technology,
Cambridge

**22** *Iris*, 1966
Acrylic on canvas/Acrylique sur toile
67 x 67 (diagonal) (170.2 x 170.2)

**23** *Lily*, 1967
Acrylic on canvas/Acrylique sur toile
68 x 136 (172.7 x 345.4)

**24** *Emérentienne*, 1967
Acrylic on canvas/Acrylique sur toile.
68 x 136 (172.7 x 345.4)

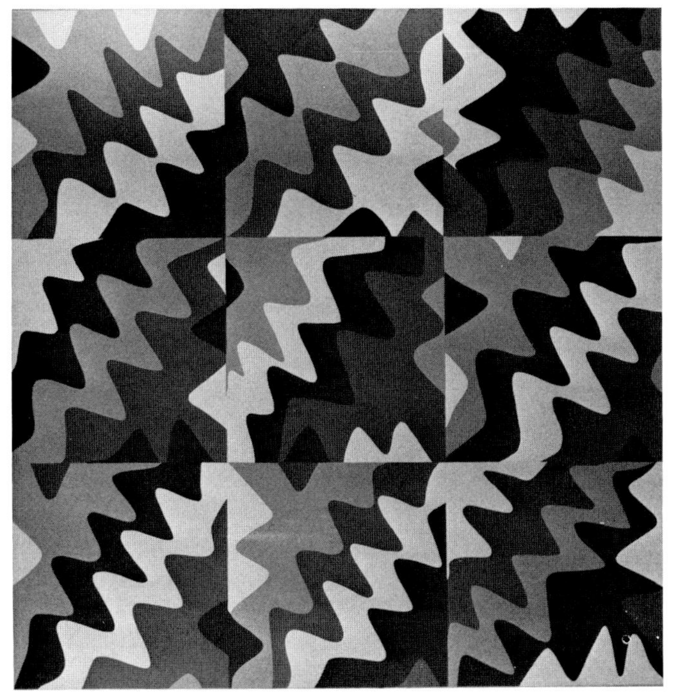

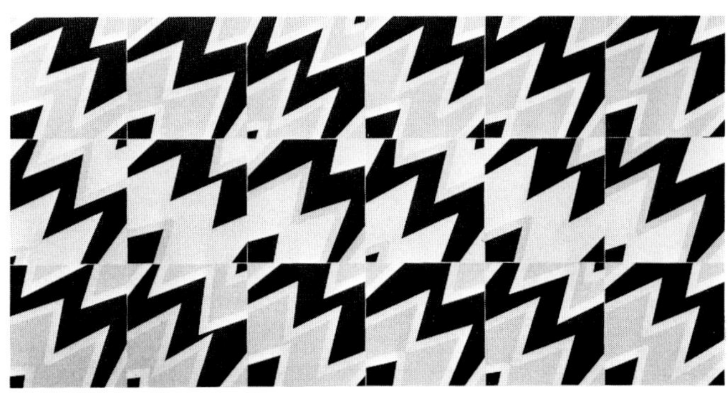

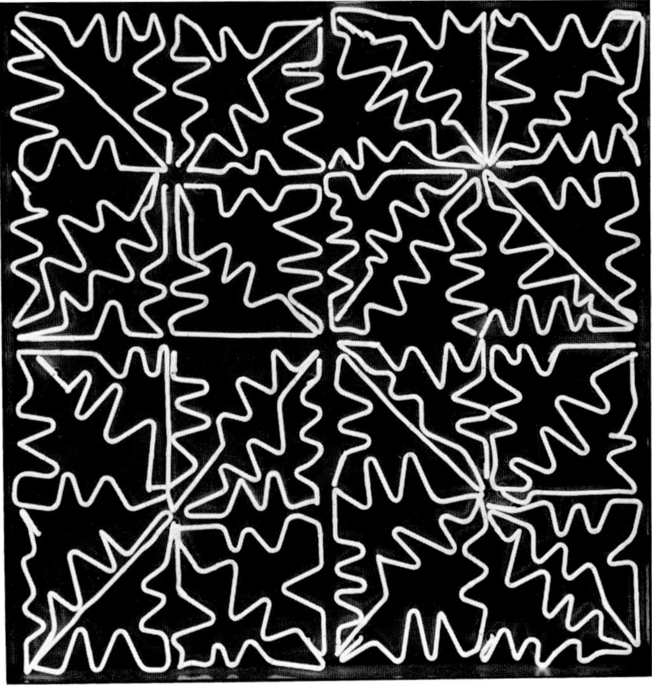

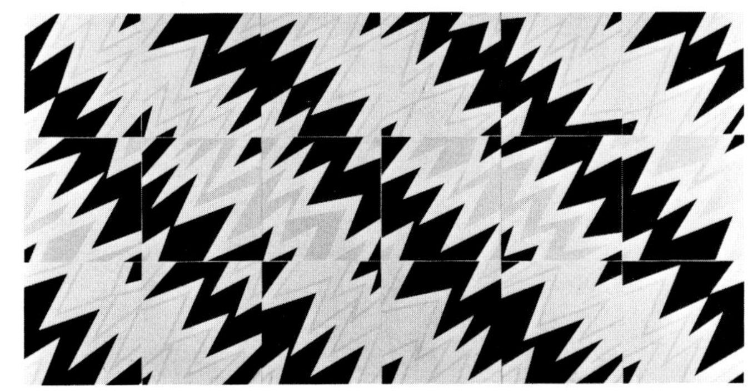



**25** *Fabiola*, 1968
Acrylic on canvas/Acrylique sur toile
80 x 80 (203.2 x 203.2)

**26** *Ciboulette*, 1968
Neon tubing and steel/Tubes de néon et acier
80 x 80 x 18 (203.2 x 203.2 x 45.7)
Collection of Musée d'art contemporain, Montreal

**27** *Marie-Thérèse*, 1970
Acrylic on canvas/Acrylique sur toile
80 x 160 (203.2 x 406.4)
Collection of the University of Regina, Norman Mackenzie Art
Gallery, Saskatchewan

**28** *Marie-Jeanne*, 1970
Acrylic on canvas/Acrylique sur toile
99 x 198 (251.5 x 503)
Collection of the Confederation Center Art Gallery and
Museum, Charlottetown, Prince Edward Island

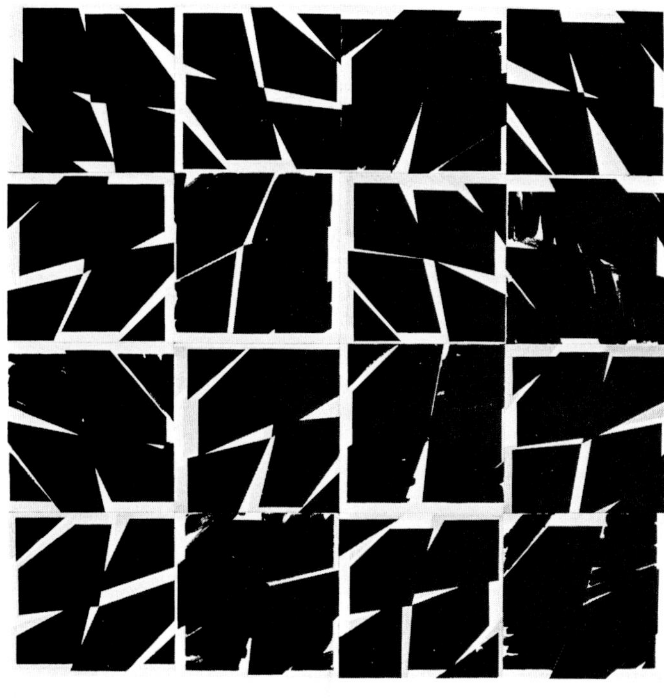

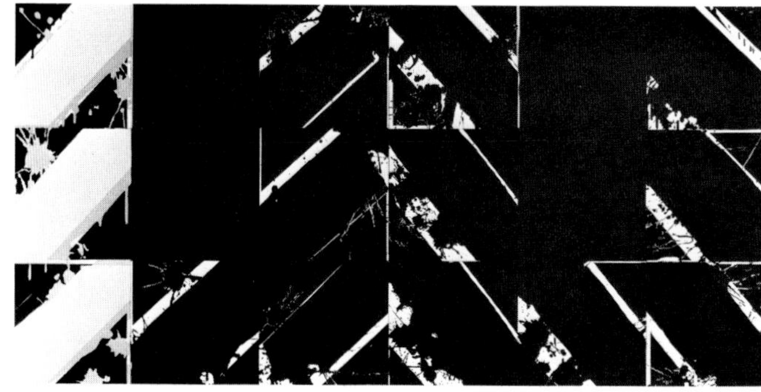

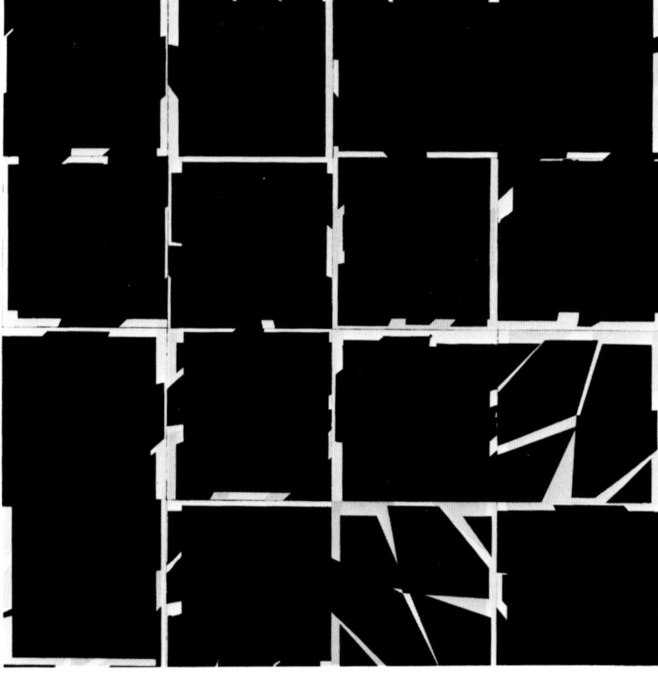

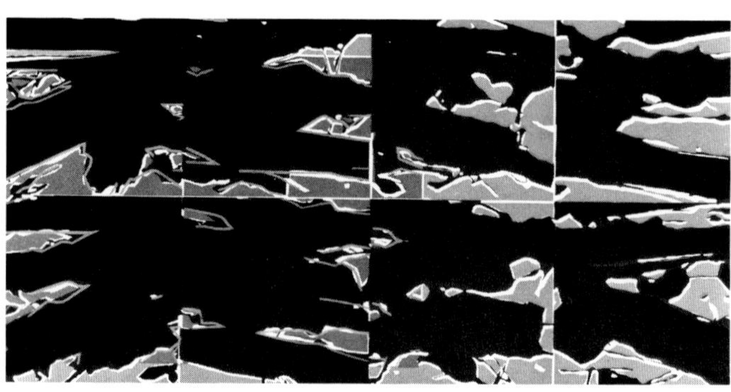

40

**29** *Nanane,* 1971
Acrylic on canvas/Acrylique sur toile
64 x 64 (162.6 x 162.6)
Collection of the City Trust, Toronto

**30** *Nénette,* 1971
Acrylic on canvas/Acrylique sur toile
64 x 64 (162.6 x 162.6)

**31** *Picotte,* 1973
Acrylic on canvas/Acrylique sur toile
36 x 72 (91.5 x 182.9)

**32** *Agatha,* 1973
Serigraph/Sérigraphie 2/30
14 x 28 (35.6 x 71.1)

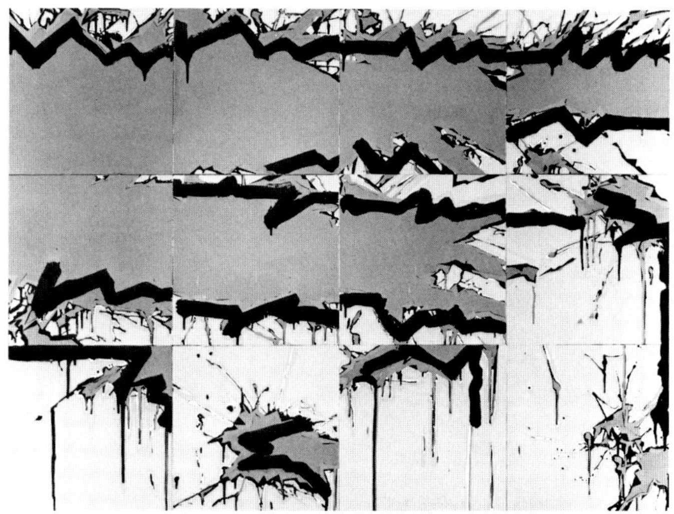

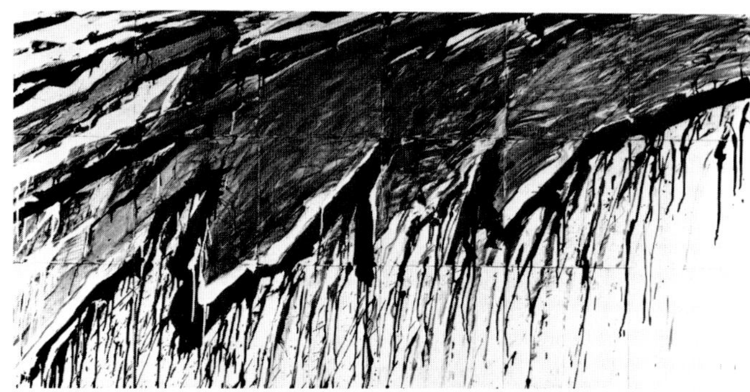

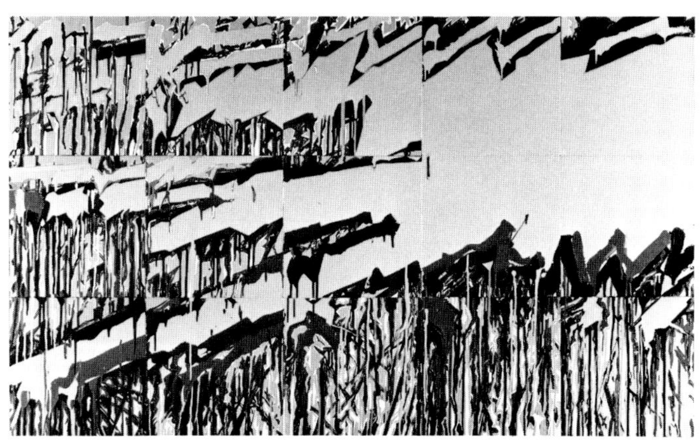

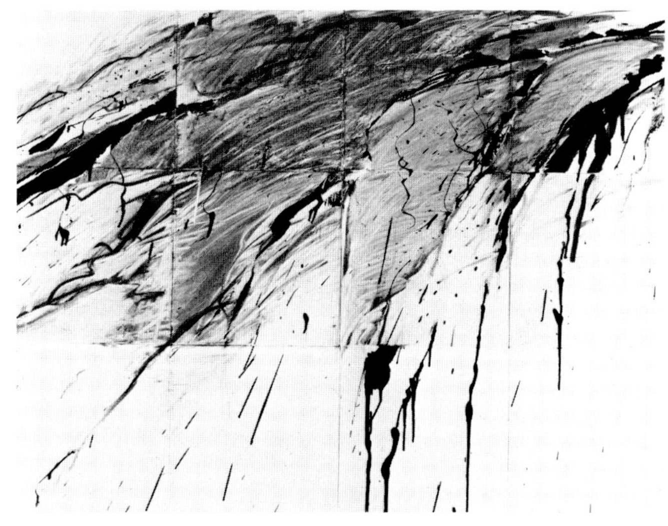

**33** *Roxie*, 1974
Acrylic on canvas/Acrylique sur toile
48 x 64 (121.9 x 162.6)

**34** *Rosarange*, 1974
Acrylic on canvas/Acrylique sur toile
48 x 80 (121.9 x 203.2)

**35** *Sapoline*, 1975
Acrylic and charcoal on canvas/Acrylique et fusain sur toile
36 x 72 (91.5 x 183)

**36** *Sibérie*, 1975
Acrylic and charcoal on canvas/Acrylique et fusain sur toile
38 x 48 (96.5 x 121.9)

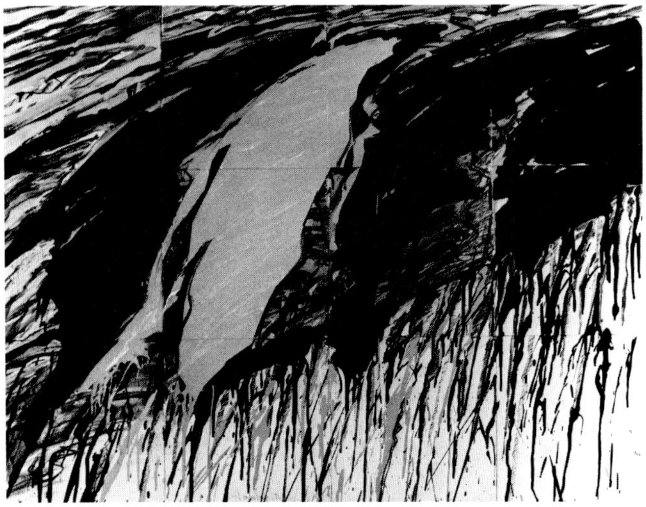

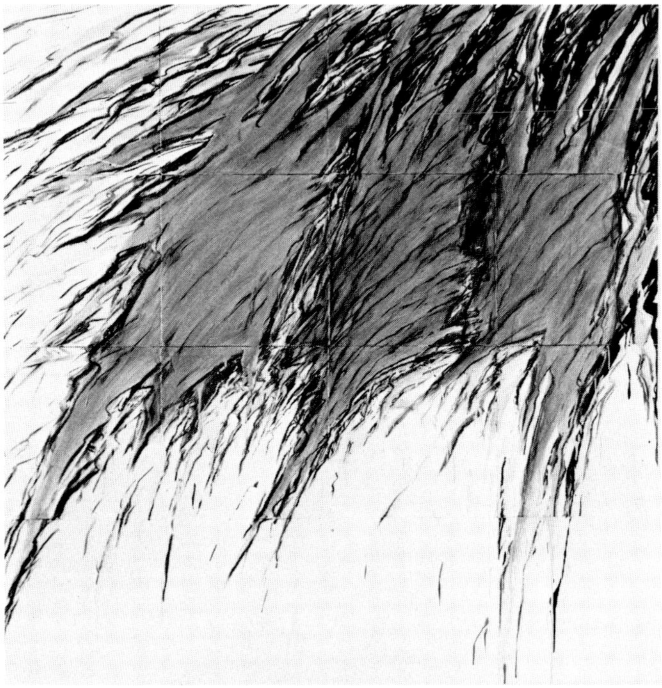

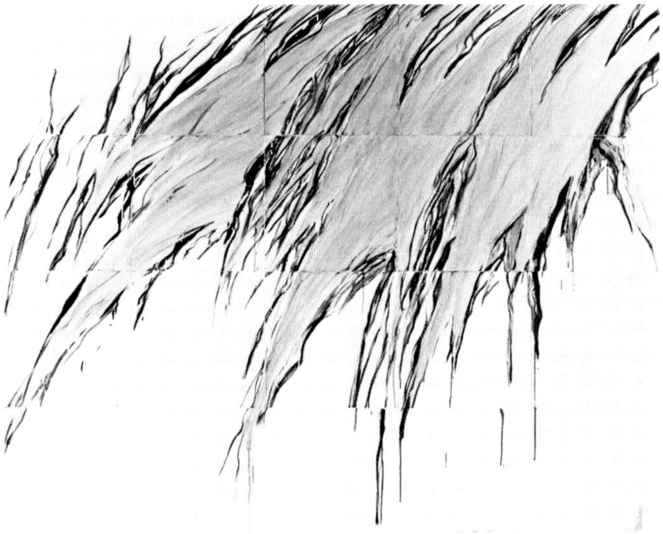

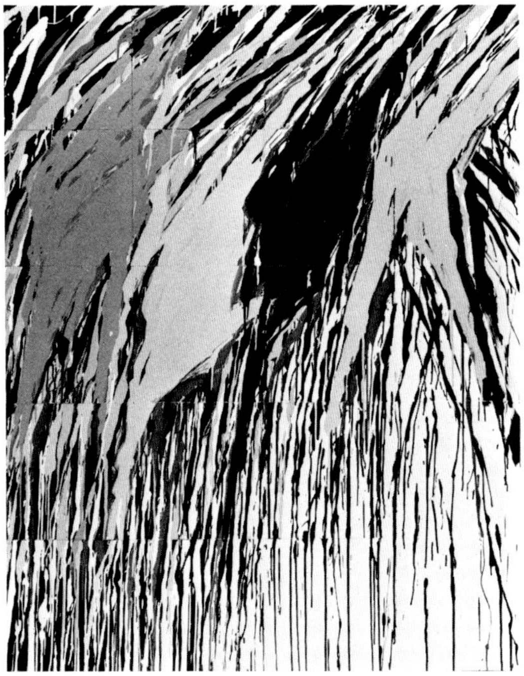

42

**37** *Taratatouille,* 1976
Acrylic and charcoal on canvas/Acrylique et fusain sur toile
36 x 48 (91.5 x 121.9)

**38** *Tanganita,* 1976
Acrylic on canvas/Acrylique sur toile
80 x 64 (203.2 x 162.6)

**39** *Tawagamie,* 1977
Acrylic and charcoal on canvas/Acrylique et fusain sur toile
64 x 64 (162.6 x 162.6)

**40** *Tawananiche,* 1977
Acrylic and charcoal on canvas/Acrylique et fusain sur toile
64 x 80 (162.6 x 203.2)

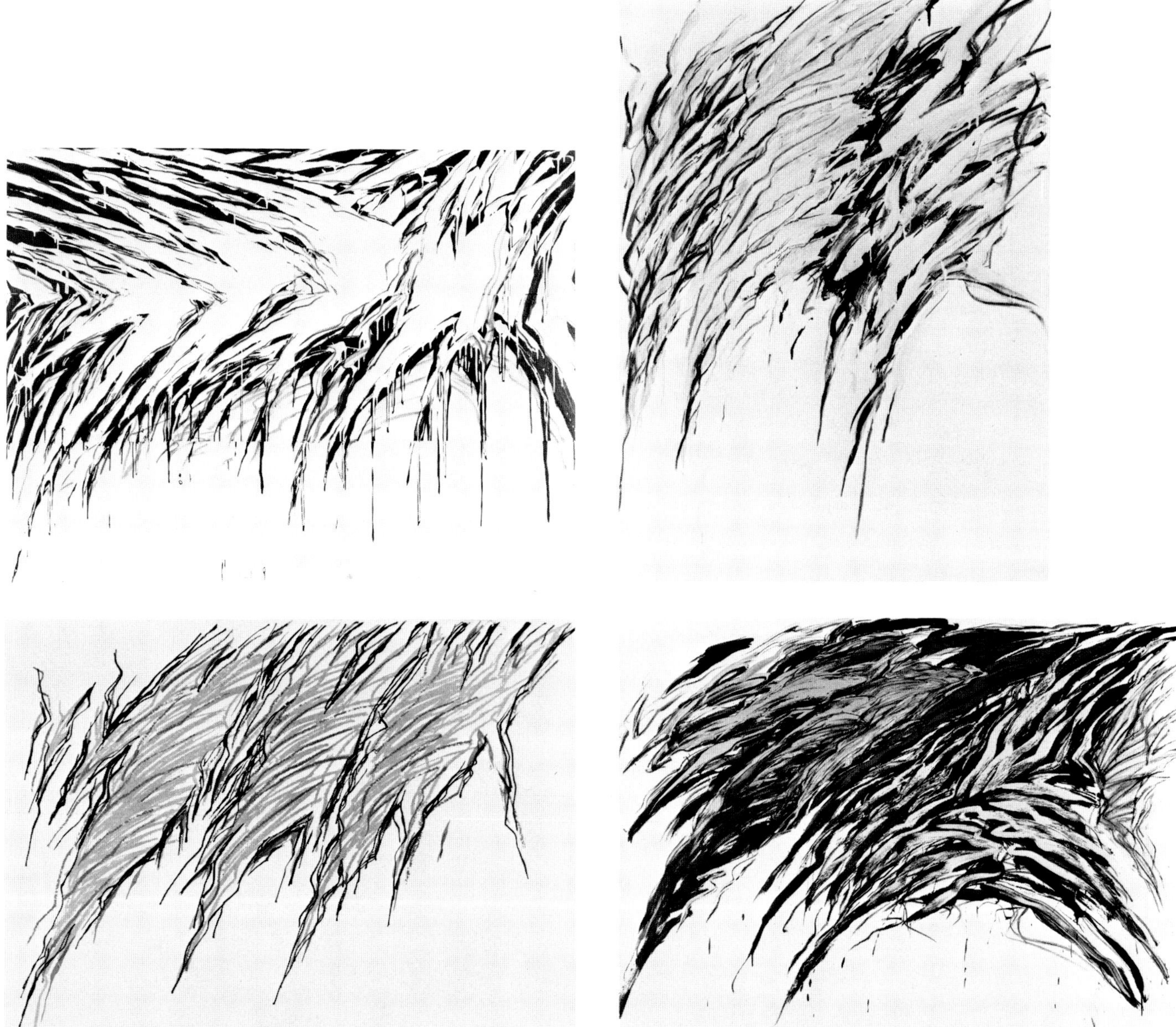



**41** *Tabetsiamite*, 1977
Acrylic and charcoal on canvas/Acrylique et fusain sur toile
72 x 96 (182.9 x 243.9)
Collection of The Canadian Council Art Bank/Collection de la
Banque d'oeuvres d'art, du Conseil des Arts du Canada,
Ottawa

**42** *Tarozita*, 1977
Serigraph/Sérigraphie 144/150
11½ x 16½ (28.6 x 41.9)

**43** *Tassiniboine*, 1977
Acrylic and charcoal on canvas/Acrylique et fusain sur toile
48 x 36 (121.9 x 91.5)
Collection of Paul E. and Thérèse Bousquet, Terrebonne

**44** *Tangara*, 1978
Acrylic and charcoal on canvas/Acrylique et fusain sur toile
61 x 81 (154.9 x 205.7)

"Debat-forum sur la peinture québécoise de 1940 à 1955." *La Presse* (Montreal), 21 June 1967, p. 72.
"Au musée d'art contemporain: 2e partie du 'Panorama de la peinture au Québec.'" *La Presse* (Montreal), 14 July 1967, p. 22.
Robillard, Yves. "'Panorama 2' beaucoup à voir peu à comprendre." *La Presse* (Montreal), 22 July 1967, p. 32.
Ayre, Robert. "Panorama of 20th century Quebec painting at Musée." *Montreal Star,* 5 August 1967, sec. Entertainments, p. 10.

Toronto, Ontario. Art Gallery of Ontario, *Perspective '67,* July 8–September 10. (Catalogue)

"The Arts." *Time* (Canada), July 14, 1967, p. 12.
Robillard, Yves. "Perspective sans audace." *La Presse* (Montreal), 15 July 1967, p. 32.

Toronto, Ontario. Dunkelman Gallery, *Art Montreal '67 Paintings and Sculptures,* September 6–30. (Catalogue)

Kritzwiser, Kay. "Five artists appear at Art Montreal '67 opening." *Globe and Mail* (Toronto), 9 September 1967, p. 15.
"No Toronto Art in Opening Show." *Telegram* (Toronto), 9 September 1967, p. 18.

São Paulo, Brazil. São Paulo Museum of Contemporary Art/Le Musée d'art contemporain de São Paulo, *O Canadà em São Paulo 1967/Le Canada à São Paulo, 1967/Canada at São Paulo 1967,* September 22–January 8, 1968, and travel: St. Catharines, Ontario. Rodman Hall Arts Center, May 10–June 2. (Catalogue)

Ostiguy, Jean-René. "Le Canada sera à São Paulo avec 2 Op: Hurtubise et Bush." *Le Devoir* (Montreal), 19 August 1967, p. 12.
"Jack Bush et Jacques Hurtubise représenteront le Canada à la 9e Biennale de São Paulo." *Le Droit* (Ottawa), 5 September 1967.
"Canadian art for Brazil show." *Citizen* (Ottawa), 9 September 1967.
Whittet, G.S. "The Bienal of São Paulo." *Art International,* November 20, 1967, pp. 36–42.
Phillips, Joan. "Paintings by Two Young Canadians On Display at Rodman Hall Show." *St. Catharines Standard* (Ontario), 10 May 1968.

Montreal, Quebec. Musée d'art contemporain, *Concours Artistique du Québec,* November 8–December 10, and travel: Quebec, Quebec. Musée du Québec, January 17–February 5, 1968.

Ste-Foy, Quebec. L'Académie de Québec, *Graphismes '67,* November 18–29.

Merler, Gracia. "Graphismes '67 à l'Académie." *Le Soleil* (Quebec), 18 November 1967, p. 30.

1968   Paris, France. Musée National d'Art Moderne, *Canada art d'aujourd'hui,* January 12–February 18, and travel: Rome, Italy. Galeria nazionale di arte moderna, May 17–June 16; Lausanne, Switzerland. Musée cantonnal des Beaux-Arts, July 15–August 25; Brussels, Belgium. Palais des Beaux-Arts, September 19–October 20. (Catalogue)

"Exposition d'art canadien à Paris." *Le Devoir* (Montreal), 6 January 1968, p. 10.
Cutler, Carol. "Paris: Canada's Americana." *International Herald Tribune* (Paris), 16 January 1968, p. 6.
Robillard, Yves. "Pourquoi les Français boudent-ils l'exposition Canadienne?." *La Presse* (Montreal), 20 January 1968, sec. Art et Lettres, p. 36.
Lamy, Laurent. "Canada Art D'Aujourd'hui à Paris." *Le Devoir* (Montreal), 27 January 1968, p. 9.
Belleau, Massue. "Ils font OP, ils font POP." *Le Magazine Maclean* (Montreal), January 1968, pp. 12–16.
Kenedy, R.C. "Paris." *Art International,* March 20, 1968, pp. 68–69.
Teyssedre, Bernard. "Canada, Art D'Aujourd'hui Musée d'Art moderne de Paris." *Vie Des Arts* (Montreal), Spring 1968, pp. 26–32.

Cambridge, Massachusetts. Hayden Gallery, Massachusetts Institute of Technology, *Seven Montreal Artists,* January 24–February 18, and travel: Washington, D.C., Washington Gallery of Modern Art. April 10–May 5. (Catalogue)

Richard, Paul. "Seven Montreal painters hold a Washington exhibition." *Montreal Star,* 27 April 1968, sec. Entertainments, p. 11.

Montreal, Quebec. Musée d'art contemporain, *10 peintres du Québec,* March 20–April 14, and travel: Quebec, Quebec. Musée du Québec, April 18–May 12. (Catalogue)

"Dix peintres du Québec au Musée d'art contemporain." *Le Devoir* (Montreal), 26 March 1968, p. 12.
Heywood, Irene. "A good Move for Contemporain." *Gazette* (Montreal), 30 March 1968, p. 52.
Bilodeau, Jean-Noël. "Dix peintres du Québec au Musée." *Le Soleil* (Quebec), 27 April 1968, p. 43.
"Informations Culturelles." *Culture Vivante* (Montreal), No. 9, 1968, p. 46.
"Musée d'Art contemporain liste des expositions." *Culture Vivante* (Montreal), No. 10, Spring 1968, p. 46.

Montreal, Quebec. Musée d'art contemporain, *Récentes acquisitions,* June 4–September 1.

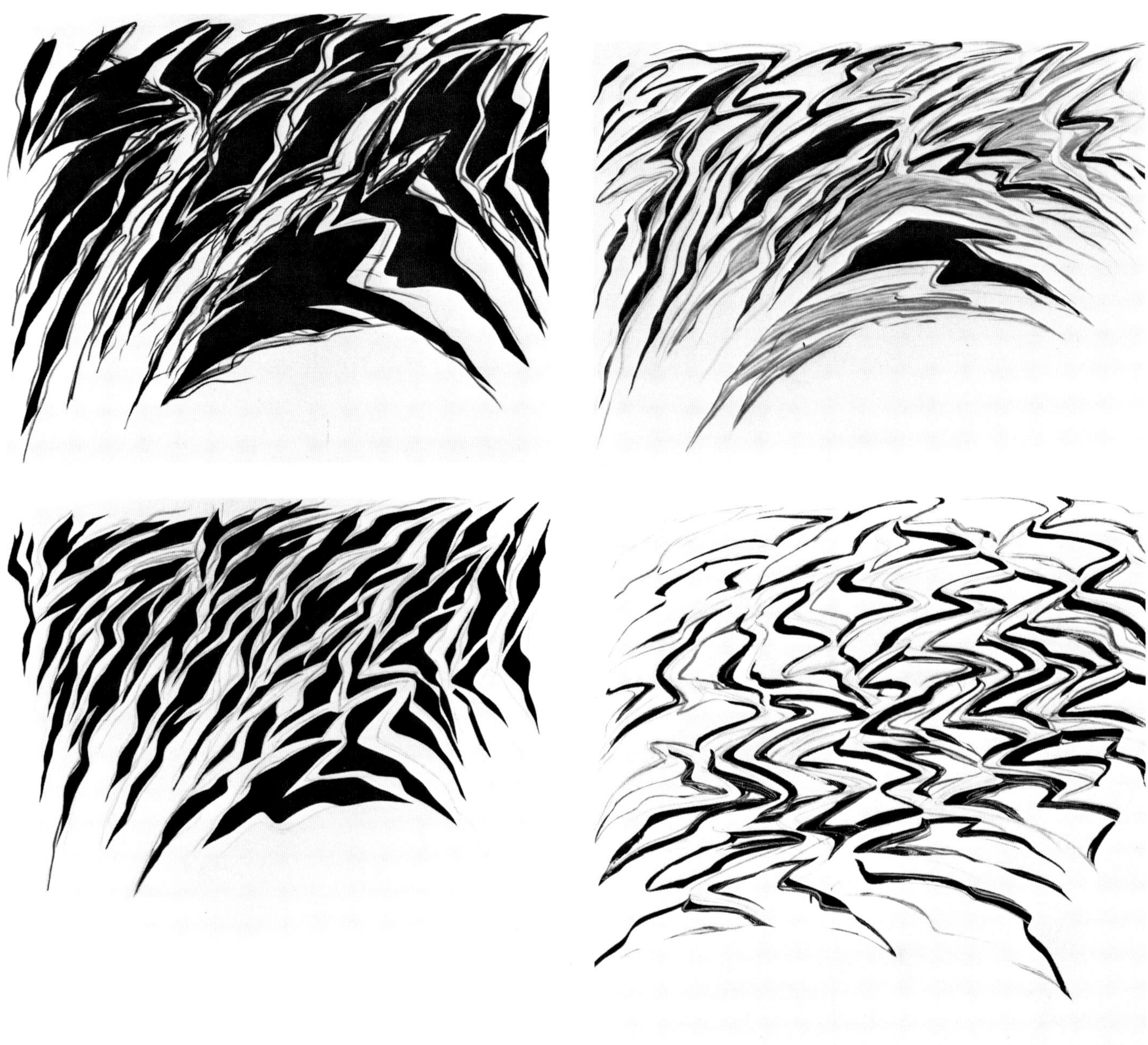



**45** *Takatanga*, 1978
Acrylic and charcoal on canvas/Acrylique et fusain sur toile
64 x 80 (162.5 x 203.2)

**46** *Tamalaya*, 1978
Acrylic and pastel on canvas/Acrylique et pastel sur toile
64 x 80 (162.5 x 203.2)

**47** *Tacocoa*, 1978
Acrylic, charcoal and pastel on canvas/Acrylique, fusain et
pastel sur toile
60 x 80 (162.5 x 203.2)

**48** *Tamimosa*, 1979
Acrylic, pastel and charcoal on canvas/Acrylique, pastel et
fusain sur toile
68 x 68 (172.7 x 172.7)

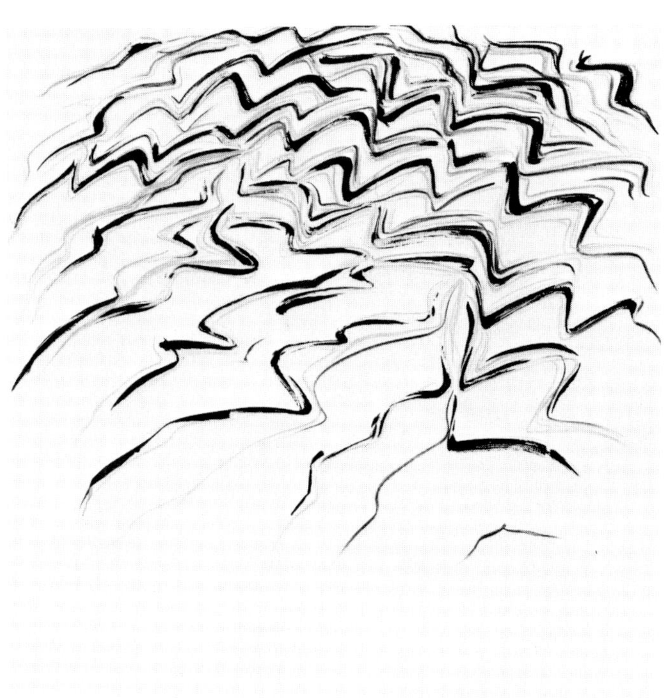 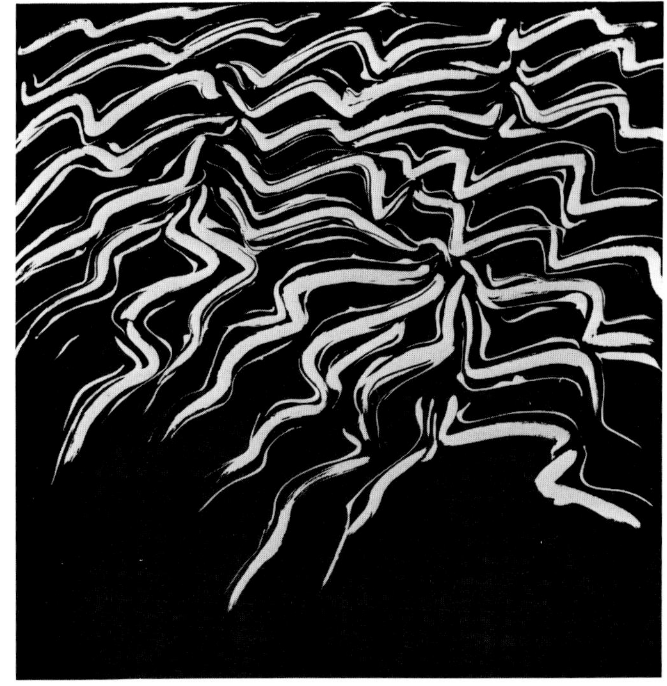

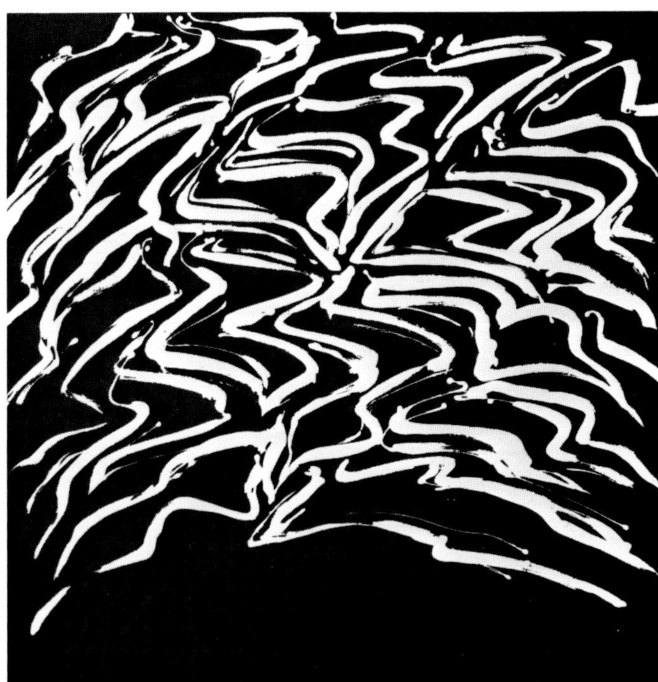 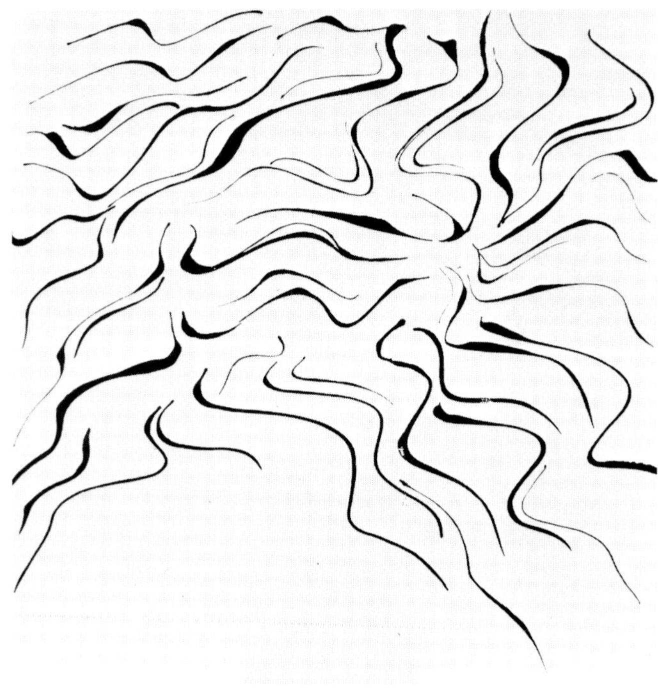



**49**  *Tafarina*, 1979
Acrylic, pastel and charcoal on canvas/Acrylic, pastel et
fusain sur toile
60 x 60 (152.4 x 152.4)

**50**  *Talulu*, 1979
Acrylic on canvas/Acrylique sur toile
50 x 50 (127 x 127)

**51**  *Tareize*, 1979
Acrylic and charcoal on canvas/Acrylique et fusain sur toile
80 x 80 (203.2 x 203.2)

**52**  *Tavirginie*, 1979
Acrylic on canvas/Acrylique sur toile
48 x 48 (121.9 x 121.9)

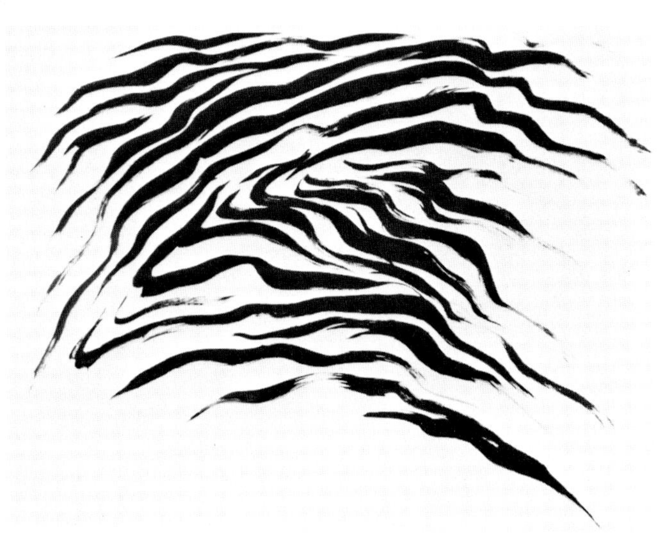
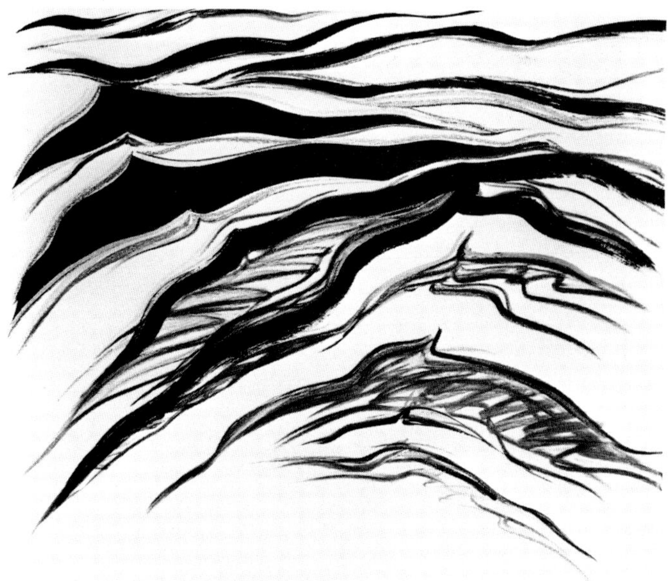
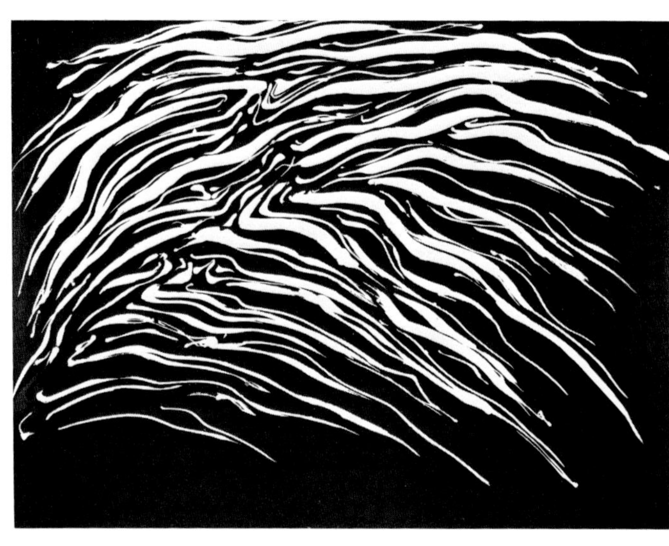
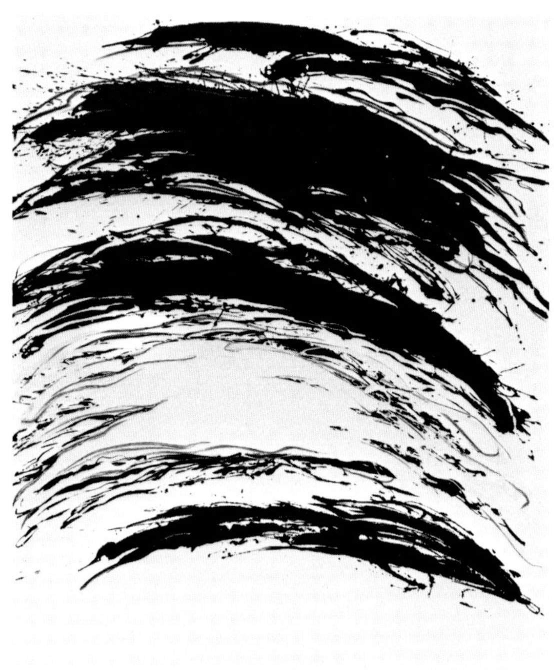

**53** *Talaska*, 1979
Acrylic on canvas/Acrylique sur toile
61 x 81 (154.9 x 205.7)

**54** *Taïda*, 1979
Acrylic on canvas/Acrylique sur toile
60 x 80 (152.4 x 203.2)

**55** *Tavanita*, 1979
Acrylic, charcoal and pastel on canvas/Acrylique, fusain et
pastel sur toile
36 x 42 (91.4 x 106.7)

**56** *Splash Sept-Cinq-Neuf*, 1980
Acrylic, charcoal and pastel on canvas/Acrylique, fusain et
pastel sur toile
80 x 67 (203.2 x 170.2)

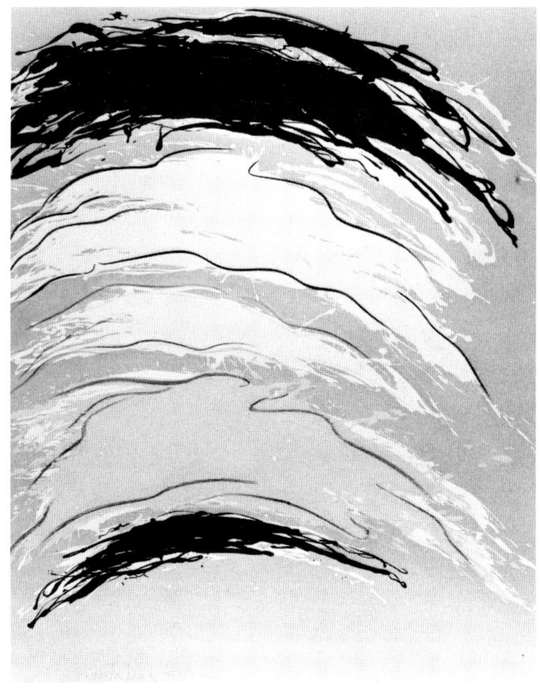

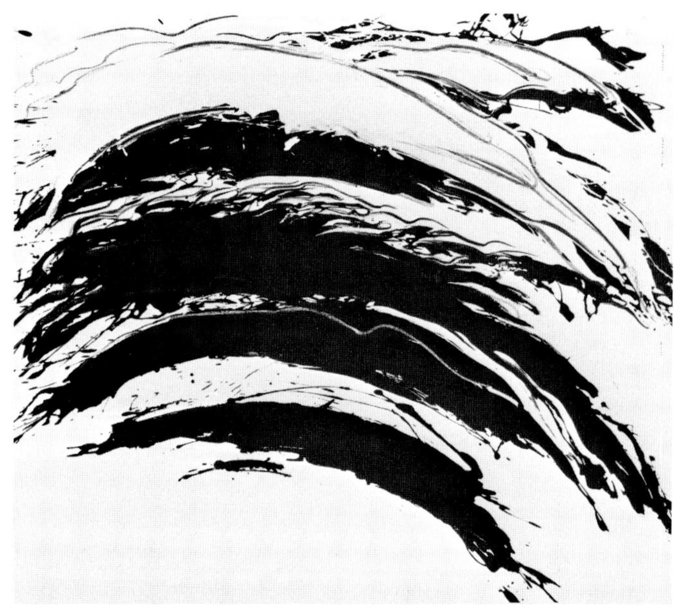

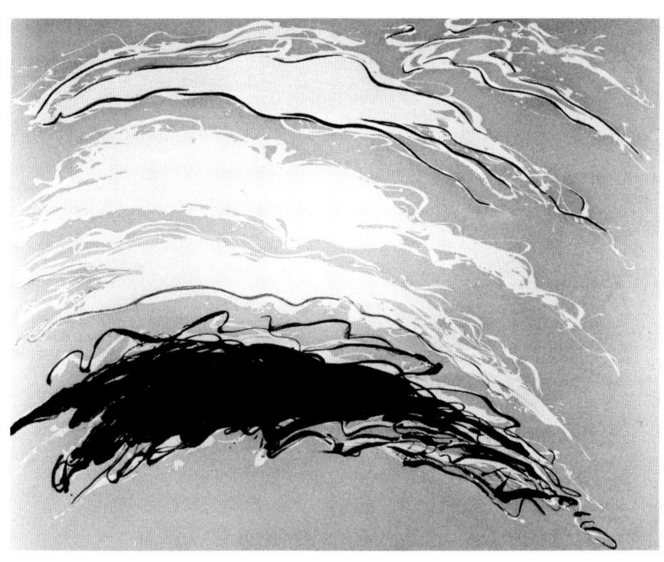

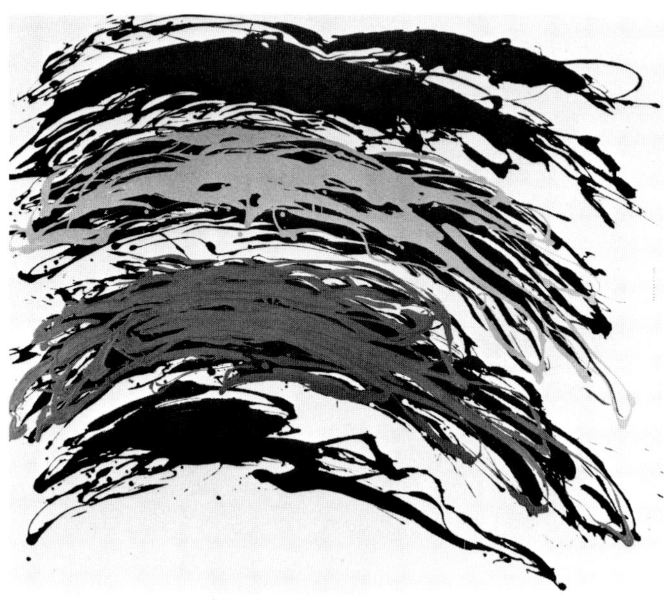



**57** *Splash Sept-Six-Zéro*, 1980
Acrylic, charcoal, pastel on canvas/Acrylique, fusain et pastel
sur toile
80 x 64 (203.2 x 162.5)

**58** *Splash Sept-Six-Un*, 1980
Acrylic, charcoal and pastel on canvas/Acrylique, fusain et
pastel sur toile
80 x 100 (203.2 x 254)

**59** *Splash Sept-Sept-Deux*, 1980
Acrylic, charcoal and pastel on canvas/Acrylique, fusain et
pastel sur toile
60 x 70 (152.4 x 177.8)

**60** *Splash Sept-Sept-Quatre*, 1980
Acrylic, charcoal and pastel on canvas/Acrylique, fusain et
pastel sur toile
60 x 70 (152.4 x 177.8)

**Exhibitions and Selected Reviews/Expositions et Bibliographie Choisie**

**One-Man/Solo**

1962    Montreal, Quebec. Galerie Denyse Delrue, *Hurtubise Oeuvres Récentes,* February 12–24.

        Lamy, Laurent. "Jacques Hurtubise à la Galerie Delrue." *Le Devoir* (Montreal), 16 February 1962, p. 8.
        Ayre, Robert. "A Tone Poet Of Rare Sensibility." *Montreal Star,* 17 February 1962, sec. Entertainments, p. 18.
        Jasmin, Claude. "Hurtubise ou l'art du barbouillage." *La Presse* (Montreal), 17 February 1962, sec. Cahier Arts et Lettres, p. 5.
        Pfeiffer, Dorothy. "Hurtubise." *Gazette* (Montreal), 17 February 1962, p. 18.

1963    Montreal, Quebec. Galerie Denyse Delrue, *Jacques Hurtubise, Oeuvres Récentes—Recent Works,* April 16–28.

        Jasmin, Claude. "Jacques Hurtubise: un art triste." *La Presse* (Montreal), 20 April 1963, sec. Cahier Arts et Lettres, p. 22.
        Lamy, Laurent. "Jacques Hurtubise, à la Galerie Denyse Delrue." *Le Devoir* (Montreal), 20 April 1963, p. 10.
        Pfeiffer, Dorothy. "At Galerie Delrue." *Gazette* (Montreal), 20 April 1963, p. 22.
        Ayre, Robert. "Brooding, Solemn Paintings Of Albert Dumouchel." *Montreal Star,* 27 April 1963, sec. Entertainments, p. 9.
        "Dans les Galeries de…" *Vie Des Arts* (Montreal), Spring 1963, p. 40.

1964    Montreal, Quebec. Galerie du Siècle, *Jacques Hurtubise Oeuvres Récentes,* May 11–24.

        Jasmin, Claude. "Hurtubise un combat étrange." *La Presse* (Montreal), 16 May 1964, sec. Cahier Arts et Lettres, p. 23.
        Lamy, Laurent. "Jacques Hurtubise, à la Galerie du Siècle." *Le Devoir* (Montreal), 16 May 1964, p. 12.
        Ayre, Robert. "Westerner and two from Quebec." *Montreal Star,* 23 May 1964, sec. Entertainments, p. 8.
        "Dans les Galeries de…" *Vie Des Arts* (Montreal), Spring 1964, p. 56.

1965    Montreal, Quebec. Galerie Nova et Vetera, Collège de Saint-Laurent, *Jacques Hurtubise, Peintures 1959–1965,* January 13–31.

        Langevin, André. "Jacques Hurtubise." *L'Alliance* (Montreal), January 1965, p. 6.

        Montreal, Quebec. Galerie du Siècle Inc., *Jacques Hurtubise,* November 15–December 5. (Pamphlet)

        Jasmin, Claude. "Jacques Hurtubise: un chirurgien du tachisme." *La Presse* (Montreal), 20 November 1965, sec. Supplément Arts et Lettres, p. 26.
        Lamy, Laurent. "Hurtubise, à la Galerie du Siècle." *Le Devoir* (Montreal), 27 November 1965, p. 15.
        "Kiyooka and Hurtubise." *Gazette* (Montreal), 4 December 1965, p. 26.
        Saint-Martin, Fernande. "Lettre de Montréal, Jacques Hurtubise." *Art International,* 20 February 1966, p. 47.

1966    New York. East Hampton Gallery. *"Jacques Hurtubise, Recent Paintings,"* July 5–22.

        Ayre, Robert. "Art Exhibitions for Summer Travellers." *Montreal Star,* 2 July 1966, sec. Entertainments, p. 8.
        Auger, Simone. "Hurtubise: Quand on a réussi à Montréal, on n'est pas rendu bien loin." *La Presse* (Montreal), 16 July 1966, sec. Cahier Arts et Lettres, pp. 13–14.

        St. John, Newfoundland. Memorial University Art Gallery, *Paintings by Jacques Hurtubise,* September 1–20.

        "Art exhibition at MUN Gallery." *The Evening Telegram,* (St. John, Newfoundland), 2 September 1966.
        Perlin, Rae. "An Inconclusive Artist?" *The Evening Telegram* (St. John, Newfoundland), 16 September 1966.

        Montreal, Quebec. Galerie du Siècle Inc., *Jacques Hurtubise,* December 6–31. (Pamphlet)

        Ayre, Robert. "Jacques Hurtubise Exhibition Sculpture by Georges Delrue." *Montreal Star,* 7 December 1966, p. 62.
        Lamy, Laurent. "Jacques Hurtubise, à la Galerie du Siècle." *Le Devoir* (Montreal), 10 December 1966, p. 12.
        Jasmin, Claude. "Hurtubise et le géométrisme." *La Presse* (Montreal), 17 December 1966, sec. Arts et Lettres, p. 21.
        MontBizon, Rea. "Art." *Gazette* (Montreal), 31 December 1966, p. 19.

1967    Hanover, New Hampshire. Dartmouth College, Hopkins Center, Beaumont-May Gallery, *Jacques Hurtubise, Artist-in-Residence,* January 3–29.

        "Canadian Art Works Show At Hop Gallery." *Dartmouth* (Hanover, New Hampshire), 6 January 1967.
        Byrd, F. "Jacques Hurtubise Hitting the Retina." *Dartmouth* (Hanover, New Hampshire), 19 January 1967.
        "Hurtubise au Dartmouth College." *La Presse* (Montreal), 15 February 1967, p. 65.

        Toronto, Ontario. The Isaacs Gallery, *Jacques Hurtubise, Recent Works,* January 11–30.



# BIBLIOGRAPHY

Hale, Barrie. "Art." *Toronto Telegram,* 11 January 1967.
"Paolozzi's graphics, Cohen's prints, and a Dine tool box."
   *Globe and Mail* (Toronto), 14 January 1967, p. 16.

New York. East Hampton Gallery, *Jacques Hurtubise,* September 16–October 7.

*New York Times,* 23 September 1967, p. 27.

Toronto, Ontario. Dunkelman Gallery, *Jacques Hurtubise,* October 23–November 11.

Kritzwiser, Kay. "Two respendent artists flash upon the city
   scene." *Globe and Mail* (Toronto), 28 October 1967, p. 25.
"Pretty Parties." *Toronto Telegram,* 2 November 1967.

1968   Ottawa, Ontario. University of Ottawa, Faculty of Arts, *Jacques
   Hurtubise,* April 24.

"Décoration à la peinture acrylite." *Le Droit* (Ottawa), 3 April
   1968, p. 5.
"Vernissage à l'Université d'Ottawa." *Le Droit* (Ottawa), 25
   April 1968, p. 5.
"University to get 4 special mural." *Ottawa Citizen,* 4 May
   1968, p. 17.

1969   Toronto, Ontario. Dunkelman Gallery, *Jacques Hurtubise Recent
   Paintings,* March 12–26.

Kritzwiser, Kay. "The salad days of Molinari and Hurtubise."
   *Globe and Mail* (Toronto), 22 March 1969, p. 22.

Montreal, Quebec. Galerie Godard Lefort, *Jacques Hurtubise,*
   October 18–November 1.

Heywood, Irene. "Pioneer: painting with lights." *Gazette*
   (Montreal), 25 October 1969, p. 45.
Thériault, Normand. "Hurtubise: 'Je suis instinctif.'" *La Presse*
   (Montreal), 25 October 1969, p. 39.
"A few shows across Canada." *Canadian Art,* October 1969,
   p. 52.
Ayre, Robert. "Entertaining in small doses." *Montreal Star,* 6
   November 1969, p. 55.

1970   Quebec, Quebec. Galerie Jolliet, *Jacques Hurtubise, Oeuvres
   Récentes,* March 7–April 14.

Allègre, Christian. "Petit journal des arts plastiques." *Le
   Devoir* (Montreal), 24 March 1970, p. 12.
Paradis, Colette L. "Une nouvelle étape dans l'oeuvre d'Hur-
   tubise." *Le Soleil* (Quebec), 4 April 1970, p. 46.
"Art World." *Montreal Star,* 25 April 1970, p. 30.

Toronto, Ontario. Carmen Lamanna Gallery, *Jacques Hurtubise,*
   October 10–29.

"Art Calendar." *Globe and Mail* (Toronto), 10 October 1970,
   p. 24.
Kritzwiser, Kay. "Realism: springboard to fancy, fantasy."
   *Globe and Mail* (Toronto), 17 October 1970, p. 32.

1971   Toronto, Ontario. Carmen Lamanna Gallery, *Jacques Hurtubise,*
   October 9–28.

Kritzwiser, Kay. "Fact-filled exhibition wide scope." *Globe and
   Mail* (Toronto), 16 October 1971, p. 32.

Sherbrooke, Quebec. Galerie d'art de l'université de Sher-
   brooke, *Jalons,* October–November, and travel: Shawinigan,
   Quebec. Salon Pic du Centre Culturel de Shawinigan;
   November 13–19; Pointe-Claire, Québec. Pointe-Claire Cul-
   tural Center, Stewart Art Gallery, September 9–23, 1972;
   St-Hyacinthe, Quebec. Galerie 051 du Séminaire de
   St-Hyacinthe, February 18–21, 1973.

"A la Galerie d'art: rétrospective des oeuvres de Jacques
   Hurtubise." *La Tribune* (Sherbrooke), 29 October 1971.
Berthiaume, René. "Le Peintre Hurtubise Fait Tache D'Encre."
   *La Tribune* (Sherbrooke), 5 November 1971, p. 9.
"Exposition Jacques Hurtubise." *Le Nouvelliste* (Trois-
   Rivières, Québec), 13 November 1971, p. 15.
"Exposition Des Oeuvres De Hurtubise." *La Voix* (Shawini-
   gan, Grand-mère), 17 November 1971, p. 23.
Pronovost, Carole. "L'exposition Hurtubise a permis au public
   de suivre l'évolution." *Le Nouvelliste* (Trois-Rivières,
   Québec), 24 November 1971, p. 52.
"Hurtubise exhibit at P.C.'s. Stewart Hall. *News and Chronicle*
   (Pointe-Claire), 14 September 1972.
"Exposition au séminaire." *Le Courrier de Saint-Hyacinthe*
   (Quebec), 14 February 1973, sec. B, p. 12.
"Hurtubise expose." *La Voix de l'Est* (Granby, Quebec), 17
   February 1973.

1972   Montreal, Quebec. Galerie Godard Multiples, *Jacques Hurtubise, graphiques et collages, / Graphics and collages by
   Jacques Hurtubise,* February 10–26.

"Calendar." *Montreal Star,* 19 February 1972, sec. C, p. 2.

Quebec, Quebec. Galerie Jolliet, *"Jacques Hurtubise,"* March.

Quebec, Quebec. Galerie Jolliet, *Hurtubise,* November 21–
   December 20.

Daigneault, Claude. "Etre Hurtubise." *Le Soleil* (Quebec), 2
   December 1972, p. 49.

Quebec, Quebec. Musée du Québec, *Hurtubise,* November
23–December 21, and travel: Montreal, Quebec. Musée d'art
contemporain, February 4–25, 1973. (catalogue)

Daigneault, Claude. *"Etre Hurtubise."* *Le Soleil* (Quebec), 2
December 1972, p. 49.
Roussan, Jacques de. "Impulsion et Rigueur de Jacques
Hurtubise." *Le Soleil* (Quebec), 3 February 1973, sec. Per-
spectives, pp. 12–13.
"Exposition Hurtubise." *Le Devoir* (Montreal), 9 February
1973, p. 15.
Arès, Françoise. "L'Evolution d'Hurtubise, au Musée d'art
Contemporain." *Le Devoir* (Montreal), 10 February 1973,
p. 20.
Bates, Catherine. "Flashes of brillance." *Montreal Star,* 10
February 1973, sec. C, p. 7.
Toupin, Gilles. "Ces tableaux à nom de femmes." *La Presse*
(Montreal), 10 February 1973, sec. D, p. 14.
Dumas, Paul. "Retrospective du peintre Jacques Hurtubise
aux musées du Québec et d'Art contemporain." *L'Informa-
tion médicale et paramédicale* (Montreal), 20 February
1973, p. 20.
Saint-Martin, Fernande. "Jacques Hurtubise." *Ateliers*
(Montreal), February 1973, pp. 1–2.
Vermette, Luce. "Rétrospective Jacques Hurtubise." *Vie Des
Arts* (Montreal), Spring 1973, p. 67.

1973   Toronto, Ontario. Marlborough Godard, *Jacques Hurtubise,* May
29–June 13.

Kritzwiser, Kay. "A color master controlling magnitude." *Globe
and Mail* (Toronto), 2 June 1973, p. 32.

Quebec, Quebec. Galerie Jolliet, *Jacques Hurtubise,*
November.

1974   Montreal, Quebec. Marlborough Godard, *Jacques Hurtubise,*
October 19–November 6.

Lehmann, Henry. "Technique: is it deadly?" *Montreal Star,* 26
October 1974, sec. D, p. 7.
Toupin, Gilles. "Hurtubise et les transes de l'Amérique." *La
Presse* (Montreal), 26 October 1974, sec. E, p. 19.
"Jacques Hurtubise." *Montréal ce mois-ci,* October 1974, pp.
17–18.
"Les Expositions." *Le Devoir* (Montréal), 2 November 1974,
p. 17.
Nixon, Virginia. "Cool and glossy people at the Moos."
*Gazette* (Montréal), 2 November 1974, p. 52.

"Jacques Hurtubise." *Québec-Presse,* 3 November 1974,
p. 27.

"ArtsCalendar." *Artscanada,* Autumn 1974, p. 87.
Pontbriand, Chantal. "Montreal, Jacques Hurtubise."
*Artscanada,* December 1974, p. 123.

1975   Quebec, Quebec. Galeria Jolliet, *Jacques Hurtubise oeuvres
récentes,* March 4–30.

Montreal, Quebec. Marlborough Godard, *Jacques Hurtubise,
Oeuvres Graphiques/Jacques Hurtubise, Recents Graphics,*
November 5–29.

Toupin, Gilles. "Jacques Hurtubise." *La Presse* (Montreal), 22
November 1975, sec. D, p. 20.

Ottawa, Ontario. Gallery Graphics, *Jacques Hurtubise,*
December.

Walker, Kathleen. "Portrait of a senior artist." *Citizen* (Ottawa),
13 December 1975, p. 76.

1976   De La Salle, Ontario. La Galerie d'art De La Salle/The Art Gallery De La Salle, *Jacques Hurtubise,* January 19–30.

"Serigraphies de Jacques Hurtubise." *Le Droit* (Ottawa), 19
January 1976, p. 16.
Bergeron, Jean-Claude. "The Art Gallery De La Salle."
*Rapport* (Ottawa), April 1976, pp. 1–3.

Quebec, Quebec. Galerie Jolliet, *Hurtubise,* October 12–
November 5.

1977   Montreal, Quebec. Galerie Gilles Gheerbrant, *Jacques
Hurtubise, peintures récentes,* April 12–30.

Leblond, Jean-Claude. "Langages de l'art: les voies de
l'imaginaire." *Le Devoir* (Montreal), 23 April 1977, p. 18.
Toupin, Gilles. "Synthèse, banalité et élégance." *La Presse*
(Montreal), 23 April 1977, sec. D, p. 19.
Lehmann, Henry, "Hurtubise breaks from past." *Montreal Star,*
27 April 1977, sec. H, p. 1.
Nixon, Virginia. "Unsober and unusual, is this art un-
Canadian?" *Gazette* (Montreal), 30 April 1977, p. 38.
Pelletier, Pierre. "Jacques Hurtubise, peintre." *Le Droit* (Ot-
tawa), 30 April 1977, pp. 17–18.
Quebec, Quebec. Galerie Jolliet, *Jacques Hurtubise,* October
12–November 5.

Tourangeau, Jean. "Trois Galeries Disparaissent et Huit Artistes Exposent." *Vie des Arts,* (Montreal), Spring 1978, pp.
70–71.

1978   Montreal, Quebec. Galerie Marielle Mailhot, *Hurtubise,*
November 3–28.

"Where it's at, Art." *Gazette* (Montreal), 10 November 1978, p. 51.

Viau, René. "Hurtubise: une peinture qui a du souffle." *Le Devoir* (Montreal), 11 November 1978, p. 30.

Toupin, Gilles. "Hurtubise: une générosité nouvelle!" *La Presse* (Montreal), 16 November 1978, sec. D, p. 8.

Nixon, Virginia. "A rare artist whose inner feelings work." *Gazette* (Montreal), 17 November 1978, p. 62.

"Art visuels." *Virus* (Montreal), November 1978, p. 19.

Desjardins, Pierre. "Jacques Hurtubise." *Artscanada*, December 1978–January 1979, p. 64.

Viau, René. "Hurtubise entre la rigueur et l'émotion." *Vie Des Arts* (Montreal), Spring 1979, p. 66.

1979   Toronto, Ontario. Gallery Moos, *Jacques Hurtubise, Paintings,* March 24–April 12.

Purdie, James. "Gallery Review." *Globe and Mail* (Toronto), 31 March 1979, sec. Third, p. 40.

Littman, Sol. "He's new one of Quebec's best." *Sunday Star* (Toronto), 1 April 1979, sec. The Arts.

Quebec, Quebec. Galerie Jolliet, *Hurtubise, dessins et tableaux récents,* April 18–May 12.

"Hurtubise." *Le Soleil* (Quebec), 14 April 1979, sec. C, p. 10.

Calgary, Alberta. Gallery Moos, Ltd., *Jacques Hurtubise, Paintings,* May 10–June 5.

Tousley, Nancy. "Visual arts." *Calgary Herald,* 17 May 1979, sec. B, p. 20.

Joyner, Brooks. "Summer art-diet fare." *Sunday Tab* (Calgary), 3 June 1979, sec. Visual Arts, p. 10.

1981   Long Beach, California. Art Museum and Galleries, California State University, Long Beach, *Hurtubise Recent Works/ Hurtubise Oeuvres Récentes,* February 9–March 14, and travel: Paris, France. Canadian Cultural Center, Canadian Embassy/Centre Culturel Canadien, Ambassade du Canada, April 3–May 31; London, England. Canada House, Canadian High Commission/Haut Commisariat du Canada, Summer; Brussels, Belgium. Canadian Embassy/Ambassade du Canada, Centre Culturel et d'information, October 31–December; Halifax, Nova Scotia. Art Gallery of Nova Scotia, January 4–February 12, 1982. (Catalogue)

Quebec, Quebec. Galerie Jolliet, *Hurtubise,* April 8–May 2.

Vancouver, British Columbia. Vancouver Art Gallery, *Hurtubise,* Summer. (Catalogue)

**Group/Groupe**

1957   Montreal, Quebec. Ile Ste-Hélène, Restaurant Hélène de Champlain, *Les moins de trente ans,* November–December 12.

Repentigny, Rodolphe de. "Deux expositions hautes en couleur." *La Presse* (Montreal), 23 November 1957, p. 66.

Saucier, Pierre. "Les promesses artistiques de demain à Hélène de Champlain." *La Patrie* (Montreal), 24 November 1957, p. 130.

"Un des 'moins de trente ans' à l'Ile." *La Presse* (Montreal), 26 November 1957, p. 31.

1958   Montreal, Quebec. Montreal Museum of Fine Arts/Musée des beaux-arts de Montréal, *75th Annual Spring Exhibition/ 75ème Salon Annuel du printemps,* March 28–April 27. (Catalogue)

1959   Montreal, Quebec. The Three Kings Studio, April 4–15.

"Artists Organize Showing." *Gazette* (Montreal), 4 April 1959, p. 11.

Montreal, Quebec. Ecole des Beaux-Arts, *Exposition de groupe,* November.

"Jacques Hurtubise Peintre." *Le Quartier Latin* (Montreal), 5 November 1959, p. 4.

1960   Montreal, Quebec. Ecole des Beaux-Arts, *La Relève,* February 5–26.

Montreal, Quebec. Ecole des Beaux-Arts, *3ème Salon de la jeune peinture,* March.

Repentigny, Françoise de. "Venor: la révélation du 3ème Salon de la jeune peinture." *Le Devoir* (Montreal), 24 March 1960, p. 7.

Sarrazin, Jean. "Promesses Tenues?" *La Presse* (Montreal), 24 March 1960, p. 38.

Montreal, Quebec. Montreal Museum of Fine Arts/Musée des beaux-arts de Montréal, *77th Annual Spring Exhibition/77ème Salon Annuel du printemps,* April 8–May 8. (Catalogue)

"Name Five to Judge Art Show." *Montreal Star,* 13 January 1963, p. 25.

1961   Montreal, Quebec. Montreal Museum of Fine Arts/Musée des beaux-arts de Montréal, Norton Gallery, *Jacques Hurtubise–Nova Taylor,* February 3–19.

"Dans les galeries." *Vie Des Arts* (Montreal), December 1960, p. 58.

"Art Notes." *Gazette* (Montreal), 4 February 1961, p. 20.
"Exposition de Nova et de Jacques Hurtubise." *Le Devoir*
    (Montreal), 6 February 1961, p. 6.
Ayre, Robert. "Canadians at a $200 Top." *Montreal Star,* 11
    February 1961, sec. Entertainment and the Arts, p. 7.
Lasnier, Yves. "Jacques Hurtubise expose au Musée des
    Beaux-Arts." *Le Devoir* (Montreal), 11 February 1961, p. 9.
Pfeiffer, Dorothy. "Art Notes." *Gazette* (Montreal), 11 February
    1961, p. 15.
Sarrazin, Jean. "Une Bonne Semaine!." *La Presse* (Montreal),
    11 February 1961, p. 22.

1962    Montreal, Quebec. Montreal Museum of Fine Arts/Musée des
        beaux-arts de Montréal, *79th Annual Spring Exhibition/
        79ème Salon Annuel du printemps,* April 7–May 6.
        (Catalogue)

        Jasmin Claude. "L'un des plus beaux salons jamais pré-
            sentés." *La Presse* (Montreal), 14 April 1962, sec. Supplé-
            ment Arts et Lettres, p. 2.

        Quebec, Quebec. Musée du Québec, *Concours Artistique de la
        Province de Québec.* August 24–September 20, and travel:
        Montreal, Quebec. Ecole des Beaux-Arts, October.

        Jasmin, Claude. "A l'école des beaux-arts, les concours ar-
            tistiques du Québec." *La Presse* (Montreal), 10 November
            1962, sec. Les beaux-arts, p. 5.

1963    Montreal, Quebec. Montreal Museum of Fine Arts/Musée des
        beaux-arts de Montréal, *80th Annual Spring Exhibition/
        80ème Salon Annuel du printemps,* April 5–May 5.
        (Catalogue)

        Pfeiffer, Dorothy. "The Spring Exhibition." *Gazette* (Montreal),
            13 April 1963, p. 25.
        "Au musée des beaux-arts, le 80ème Salon du printemps."
            *La Presse* (Montreal), 20 April 1963, sec. Supplément arts
            et lettres, p. 23.

        Ottawa, Ontario. The National Gallery of Canada/Galerie
        nationale du Canada, *5th Biennial Exhibition of Canadian
        Painting/5E Exposition Biennale De La Peinture Canadienne,*
        September 20–November 2, 1963, and travel: Quebec,
        Quebec. Musée du Québec, April 23–May 10, 1964; Victoria,
        British Columbia. Art Gallery of Greater Victoria, May 19–
        June 7. (Catalogue)

        Lamy, Laurent. "Expositions à venir à la Galerie nationale." *Le
            Devoir* (Montreal), 12 January 1963, p. 10.
        Lambert, Helen. "The Last Works of Nicolas de Stael." *New
            York Herald Tribune* (Paris), 19 June 1963, p. 10.

Montreal, Quebec. Ecole des Beaux-Arts, *Concours Artistique
de la Province de Québec,* October 21–November 2, and
travel: Quebec, Quebec. Musée du Québec, December 27–
February 2, 1964.

1964    Montreal, Quebec. Galerie du Siècle, *Dynamisme '64',* March
        16–29.

        Lamy, Laurent. "Expositions de groupe, chez Camille Hébert
            et à la Galerie du Siècle." *Le Devoir* (Montreal), 21 March
            1964, p. 14.
        Jasmin, Claude. "Deux expos collectives à ne pas manquer."
            *La Presse* (Montreal), 28 March 1964, p. 23.

        Montreal, Quebec. Montreal Museum of Fine Arts/Musée des
        beaux-arts de Montréal, *81st Annual Spring Exhibition/81ème
        Salon Annuel du printemps,* April 8–May 3. (Catalogue)

        Ottawa, Ontario. The National Gallery of Canada/Galerie
        nationale du Canada, *Canadian Water Colours, Drawings and
        Prints 1964/Aquarelles, estampes et dessins canadiens 1964,*
        June 5–September 7, and travel: Kingston, Ontario. Agnès
        Etherington Art Center, September 18 –October 12; Halifax,
        Nova Scotia. Nova Scotia College of Art, October 23–
        November 15; Calgary, Alberta. Calgary Allied Arts Center,
        November 27–December 27; Saskatoon, Saskatchewan.
        Saskatoon Art Center, January 15–February 7, 1965; St-John,
        New Brunswick. New Brunswick Museum, February 19–
        March 14; Vancouver, British Columbia. University of British
        Columbia, March 26–April 19; Victoria, British Columbia. Art
        Gallery of Greater Victoria, April 30–May 23. (Catalogue)

        Weiselberger, Carl. "At National Gallery, A shower of impor-
            tant art exhibits for summer tourists and Ottawans." *Ottawa
            Citizen* (Ontario), 6 June 1964, sec. Entertainment, p. 4.
        Kritzwiser, Kay. "An unusual point of view by Canada's art-
            ists." *Globe and Mail* (Toronto), 4 July 1964, p. 13.

        Montreal, Quebec. The Sir George Williams University, *The Sir
        George Williams University Collection of Canadian Art Ac-
        quisitions 1964,* October 4–23. (Catalogue)

        Quebec, Quebec. Musée du Québec, *Concours Artistiques du
        Québec,* October 7–26, and travel: Montreal, Quebec. Institut
        des arts appliqués, November 11–30.

1965    Ottawa, Ontario. The National Gallery of Canada/Galerie
        nationale du Canada, *Paintings by Young Quebec Artists/
        Oeuvres de jeunes peintres du Québec,* February, and travel:
        Western Canada Art Circuit. (Catalogue)

        Toronto, Ontario. Jerrold Morris International Gallery, *Paintings
        Barbeau, Hurtubise, Sculpture Manolo,* February 6–20, 1965.

Kritzwiser, Kay. "Manolo Reflects Streets of Paris, Madrid."
*Globe and Mail* (Toronto), 6 February 1965, p. 15.

Kingston, Ontario. Agnès Etherington Art Center, Queen's University, *New Trends in Canadian Painting,* March 7–28.
(Catalogue)

Montreal, Quebec. Montreal Museum of Fine Arts/Musée des
beaux-arts de Montréal, *82nd Annual Spring Exhibition/
82ème Salon Annuel du printemps,* April 9–May 9.
(Catalogue)

"Le musée des B.A. achètera des oeuvres exposées *au
salon du printemps.*" *Le Devoir* (Montreal), 1 May 1965,
. p. 17.
Robillard, Yves. "82ème Salon annuel du Printemps." *Vie Des
Arts* (Montreal), Summer 1965, pp. 34–39.

Montreal, Quebec. La Galerie du Siecle, *Petits Formats,* May
17–29.

Jasmin, Claude. "De la profusion des moyens d'expressions." *La Presse* (Montreal), 22 May 1965, p. 23.
Montbizon, Rea. "En Petit Format." *Gazette* (Montreal), 22
May 1965, p. 26.
Jasmin, Claude. "Toccate et fugues de Molinari, Hurtubise et
Tousignant sur des airs connus." *La Presse* (Montreal), 29
May 1965, sec. Arts et Lettres, pp. 22–23.

Ottawa, Ontario. The National Gallery of Canada/Galerie
nationale du Canada, *Sixth Biennial Exhibition of Canadian
Painting 1965/Sixième Exposition biennale de la peinture
canadienne 1965,* June 4–August 22, and travel: Fredericton,
New Brunswick. Beaverbrook Art Gallery, September 8–October 3; Montreal, Quebec. Musée d'art contemporain, October
21–November 14; London, Ontario. Public Library and Art
Museum, November 26–December 19; Regina, Saskatchewan. Norman Mackenzie Art Gallery, January 7–February 6,
1966; Edmonton, Alberta. Edmonton Art Gallery, February 23–
March 20. (Catalogue)

Ayre, Robert. "Sixth Canadian Biennial Opens in Ottawa."
*Montreal Star,* 12 June 1965, sec. Entertainments, p. 10.
"Sask. painters prominent in national art exhibition." *Regina
Leader Post* (Saskatchewan), 16 June 1965.
"Canada." *Time* (Canada), June 18, 1965, pp. 9–12.
Montbizon, Rea. "Canadian Painting 1965—A Shift In Focus."
*Gazette* (Montreal), 19 June 1965, sec. Entertainments, p. 24.
Weiselberger, Carl. "Did make-up hobgoblins interfere with
Ottawa artist's success?" *Citizen* (Ottawa), 26 June 1965,
sec. Entertainment, p. 4.

Dexter, Gail. "New names, ideas steal show." *Daily Star*
(Toronto), 21 August 1965.
Ostiguy, Jean-René. "La sixième biennale de la peinture
canadienne." *Vie Des Arts* (Montreal), Summer 1965,
pp. 22–27.
Watmough, David. "Sixth Biennial exhibition victim of time's
corrosion." *Sun* (Vancouver), 9 April 1966.
Watkins, Ralph. The Sixth Biennial of Canadian Painting. *Free
Press* (Winnipeg), 20 May 1966.

Montreal, Quebec. Musée d'art contemporain, *Artistes de
Montréal,* July 12–August 22. (Catalogue)

"Dans les Galeries de…" *Vie Des Arts* (Montreal), Summer
1965, p. 57.
"Le Musée D'Art Contemporain." *Vie Des Arts* (Montreal), Autumn, 1965, pp. 47–48.

Ottawa, Ontario. The National Gallery of Canada./Galerie
Nationale du Canada, *Montreal Artists, 1965–1966/Artistes de
Montréal, 1965–1966,* and travel: Regina, Alberta. Norman
Mackenzie Art Gallery, September 3–26; Saskatoon, Saskatchewan. Saskatoon Art Center, October 8–31; Winnipeg,
Manitoba. Winnipeg Art Gallery Association, November 12–
December 5; New Brunswick. Dalhousie University,
January 7–30, 1966; Sackville, New Brunswick. Mount Allison
University, February 11–March 6; Fredericton, Alberta. Beaverbrook Art Gallery, March 15–April 12. (Catalogue)

São Paulo, Brazil. São Paulo Museum of Contemporary Art/
Musée d'art contemporian de São Paulo, *O Canadá em São
Paulo 1965/Canada at São Paulo 1965/Le Canada à São
Paulo 1965,* September 4–November 28, and travel: Ottawa,
Saskatoon, Winnipeg, Kingston. (Catalogue)

Basile, Jean. "Bientôt à la biennale de São Paulo Tousignant
et Hurtubise exprimeront une 'nouvelle sensibilité'
québécoise." *Le Devoir* (Montreal), 22 May 1965, p. 11.
"A la Biennale de São Paulo mention obtenue par Roy
Kiyooka." *Le Devoir* (Montreal), 9 September 1965, p. 6.
"Entre Parenthèses." *La Presse* (Montreal), 10 September
1965, p. 16.

Quebec, Quebec. Musée du Québec, *Concours Artistique du
Québec,* September 9–17 and travel: Montreal, Quebec.
Musé d'art contemporain, September 28–October 17.

"Hurtubise et Soucy lauréats des Concours artistiques du
Québec." *La Presse* (Montreal), 10 September 1965, p. 16.
Lamy, Laurent. "En marge de l'attribution des prix, Un choix
significatif." *Le Devoir* (Montreal), 10 September 1965, p. 6.
_________ . "Pierre Laporte annonce hier à Québec les prix

beaux-arts de la province." *Le Devoir* (Montreal), 10 September 1965, p. 6.
"Les Lauréats." *La Presse* (Montreal), 11 September 1965, p. 23.
O'Neil, Jean. "Les Concours artistiques: on s'est efforcé de retenir la crème…" *La Presse* (Montreal), 11 September 1965, sec. Arts et Lettres, p. 23.
"21e vernissage des concours du Québec." *Le Droit* (Ottawa), 11 September 1965, p. 14.
Ayre, Robert. "Quebec's Concours Artistique, 1965." *Montreal Star,* 2 October 1965, sec. Entertainments, p. 12.

New York. New York Hilton Art Gallery, *International Art Festival,* November 17–February 15, 1966.

1966  Montreal, Quebec. Musée d'art contemporain, *Collections,* January 6–February 13.

Quebec, Quebec. Musée du Québec, *Vingt-cinq ans de libération de l'oeil et du geste,* February 22–March 27. (Catalogue)

Derome, Gilles. "Peinture." *Le Devoir* (Montreal), 1 April 1967, p. 13.

Quebec, Quebec. Musée du Québec, *Concours Artistiques du Québec,* May 4–23, and travel: Montreal, Quebec. Musée d'art contemporain, September 8–22.

Robillard, Yves. "Au contemporain les élus des Concours artistiques du Québec." *La Presse* (Montreal), 17 September 1966, p. 2.

Mount Orford Park. The Mount Orford Art Gallery, *Group Show,* June 24–July 8.

Ayre, Robert. "Art exhibition for summer travellers." *Montreal Star,* 2 July 1966, sec. Entertainments, p. 8.

Winnipeg, Manitoba. The Winnipeg Art Gallery, *The Tenth Winnipeg Show,* November 5–30. (Catalogue)

"The 10th Winnipeg Show." *Free Press* (Winnipeg), 4 November 1966.
"Art Show Saturday." *Free Press* (Winnipeg), 5 November 1966.

Montreal, Quebec. Musée d'art contemporain, *Guild Graphique,* December 1–January 1967.

Montbizan, Rea. "Art." *Gazette* (Montreal), 31 December 1966, p. 19.

54    1967  Kitchener, Ontario. Kitchener-Waterloo Art Gallery, *Centennial*

*Exhibition of Quebec and Ontario Contemporary Painters, 1967,* February 4–26, and travel: Guelph, Ontario. University of Guelph, March 10–26; Sarnia, Ontario. Sarnia Public Library and Art Gallery, April 7–29; London, Ontario. London Public Library and Art Museum, May 5–30; Toronto, Ontario. York University, June 2–30; Owen Sound, Ontario. Tom Thomson, Memorial Art Gallery, July 7–August 31; Windsor, Ontario. Willistead Art Gallery, September 5–28; Kingston, Ontario. Agnès Etherington Art Center, Queen's University, October 8–29; St. Catharines, Ontario. Rodman Hall, November 3–26; Woodstock, Ontario. Oxford County Art Association, December 1–31. (Catalogue)

"Centennial Art Show to Open in K-W." *Kitchener-Waterloo Record* (Ontario), 20 January 1967.
"Post-Dinner Parties Mark Gala Opening." *Kitchener-Waterloo Record* (Ontario), 4 February 1967, p. 26.
Zaritsky, John. Centennial Art Show Opening Proves 'Real Gas.'" *Kitchener-Waterloo Record* (Ontario), 6 February 1967.

Montreal, Quebec. Musée d'art contemporain, *Acquisitions 1966.* February 28–March 19.

Ottawa, Ontario. The National Gallery of Canada./Galerie nationale du Canada, *Three Hundred Years of Canadian Art/ Trois cents ans d'art canadien,* May 12–September 17, and travel. (Catalogue)

Weiselberger, Carl. "Is Canada a young country?" *Ottawa Citizen,* 12 May 1967, p. 21.
Krîtzwiser, Kay. "Easel to OP–300 Years of Canadian Art." *Globe and Mail* (Toronto), 13 May 1967, sec. Globe Magazine, pp. 11–14.
Ayre, Robert. "300 years of Art." *Montreal Star,* 20 May 1967, p. 5.
Robillard, Yves. "Que s'est-il passé *au Canada en 300 ans?.*" *La Presse* (Montreal), 17 June 1967.
Bilodeau, Jean Noël. "Cent années de peinture canadienne." *Le Soleil* (Quebec), 23 March 1968, p. 30.

Boston, Massachusetts. Institute of Contemporary Art, *Nine Canadians,* May 19–June 21. (Catalogue)

Montreal, Quebec. Musée d'art contemporain, *Panorama de la peinture au Québec 1940–1966,* May 26–August 20. (Catalogue)

Robillard, Yves. "Toute l'histoire de la peinture québécoise en une rétrospective passionnante." *La Presse* (Montreal), 27 May 1967, p. 41.
Lamy, Laurent. "Panorama I et II." *Le Devoir* (Montreal), 10 June 1967, p. 13.

Ottawa, Ontario. The National Gallery of Canada./Galerie
nationale du Canada, *Seventh Biennial of Canadian
Painting/Septième Biennale de la peinture canadienne,* July
4–September 2. (Catalogue)

Andrews, Bernadette. "The Biennial." *Telegram* (Toronto), 6 July
1968, p. 54.
Kritzwiser, Kay. "The Biennial: the fruit of a search for Canadian
works." *Globe and Mail* (Toronto), 6 July 1968, p. 25.
Charpentier, Fulgence. "Une biennale dans le vent." *Le Droit*
(Ottawa), 10 July 1968.
Ayre, Robert. "VII Canadian Biennial, Vitality and diversity."
*Montreal Star,* 13 July 1968.
Thériault, Normand. "Diversité et éparpillement à la Biennale
canadienne." *La Presse* (Montreal), 27 July 1968, sec.
Cahier 3, p.32.
Robillard, Yves. "L'imagination au pouvoir!" *La Presse*
(Montreal), 24 August 1968.
Lamy, Laurent. "Septième Biennale De la Peinture Canadienne."
*Vie Des Arts* (Montreal), Autumn 1968.

Edinburgh, Scotland. Edinburgh College of Art, *Canada 101
Edinburgh International Festival,* August 18–September 7.
(Catalogue)

"Les artistes canadiens au festival d'Edimbourg." *Le Devoir*
(Montreal), 1 February 1968, p. 10.
"Art canadien à Edimbourg." *Le Devoir* (Montreal), 15 April 1968,
p. 10.

"Jugée 'blessante' une oeuvre d'art canadienne est retirée
de l'exposition d'Edimbourg." *Le Devoir* (Montreal), 20
August 1968, p. 12.
"Exposition d'oeuvres canadiennes à Edimbourg." *La Presse*
(Montreal), 21 August 1968, p. 66.
"Exposition d'Edimbourg critique élogieuse." *Le Devoir*
(Montreal), 22 August 1968, p. 10.

Montreal, Quebec. Montreal Museum of Fine Arts/Musée des
beaux-arts de Montréal, *The Art Gallery in the factory/Le
Musée dans l'usine,* September 10–October 6, and travel.
(Catalogue)

Thériault, Normand. "Quoi de neuf à l'usine? Des tableaux."
*La Presse* (Montreal), 7 September 1968, p. 41.
"Un musée dans l'usine." *Le Devoir* (Montreal), 7 September
1968, p. 13.

Winnipeg, Manitoba. The Winnipeg Art Gallery, *The Eleventh
Winnipeg Show,* October 30–November 24. (Catalogue)

Montreal, Quebec. Eaton, *The Hadassah Collection/La collection Hadassah,* November 16–25, and travel: Montreal,
Quebec. Windsor Hotel, November 26.

Ballantyne, Michael. "Thomas More, Hadassah shows."
*Montreal Star,* 16 November 1968, sec. Entertainments,
p. 15.

Quebec, Quebec. Musée du Québec, *Concours Artistique du
Québec,* November 22–December 12, and travel: Montreal,
Quebec. Musée d'art contemporain, February 19–March 16,
1969.

"Informations Culturelles." *Culture Vivante* (Montreal), No. 7/8,
1968.

Toronto, Ontario. Art Gallery of Ontario, *Canadian Artists 68/
Artistes canadiens 68,* November 30–December 29.
(Catalogue)

Hamilton, Ontario. Art Gallery of Hamilton. *Eighty-Ninth Annual
Exhibition Royal Canadian Academy of Arts/89E Exposition
Annuelle Academie Royale des Arts du Canada,* December
7–January 15, 1969, and travel: Edmonton, Alberta. Edmonton
Art Gallery, February 13–March 9. (Catalogue)

Cambridge, Massachusetts. Massachusetts Institute of
Technology. *The MIT Art Collection.* (Catalogue)

1969   Ottawa, Ontario. The Ottawa Section of the National Council of
Jewish Women of Canada, *Exhibition and Sale of Works by
Leading Canadian Artists from Coast to Coast,* March 31.
(Catalogue)

Montreal, Quebec. Australian Pavilion, Man and His World/
Pavillon Australien, Terre des Hommes, *Art Today/Art d'aujourd'hui,* June 12–September 7. (Catalogue)

Montreal, Quebec. Galerie Godard Lefort, *Exposition de
groupe,* Summer 1969.

Lowndes, Joan. "Hurtubise joins the electric world of the
kinetic sculptors." *Vancouver Province,* 24 July 1969.

Ottawa, Ontario. The National Gallery of Canada/Galerie
nationale du Canada, *The Canada Council Collection/
Collection du Conseil des Arts du Canada, 1969,* and travel:
Montreal, Quebec. Montreal Museum of Fine Arts/Musée
des beaux-arts de Montréal, August 20–September 20.
(Catalogue)

"Des oeuvres canadiennes au musée des beaux arts." *Le
Devoir* (Montreal), 12 August 1970, p. 8.

Toronto, Ontario. Carmen Lamanna Gallery, *Canadian Electric
Company,* December 11–27.

Toronto, Ontario. Carmen Lamanna Gallery, *North American Vibrations,* December 30–January 20, 1970.

Lord, Barry. "Canada didn't lose this one anyway." *Toronto Daily Star,* 2 January 1970.
Kritzwiser, Kay. "Bloore: no short cuts on the road to purity." *Globe and Mail* (Toronto), 10 January 1970, p. 24.

1970    Montreal, Quebec. Musée d'art contemporain. *Grand Formats,* January 22–February 15. (Catalogue)

"Une expo importante: 'Grands Formats.'" *Le Devoir* (Montreal), 20 January 1970, p. 10.
Benoit, André Luc. "Du 'jongle-nouille' de Cozic au 'Duo-reflex' de Tousignant." *Le Devoir* (Montreal), 28 January 1970, p. 10.
"Artistes de Montréal au Musée d'art contemporain." *Le Droit* (Ottawa), 30 January 1970, p. 23.
Benoit, André Luc. "De grands formats...mais à la dimension de qui?." *Le Devoir* (Montreal), 31 January 1970, p. 17.
Bardo, Arthur. "Local artists exhibit large format paintings." *Montreal Star,* 5 February 1970, p. 28.
Heywood, Irene. "Paintings, like life, grow larger." *Gazette* (Montreal), 7 March 1970, p. 47.

Ottawa, Ontario. The National Gallery of Canada/Galerie nationale du Canada, *Ninetieth Annual Exhibition Royal Canadian Academy of Arts/Quatre-vingt-dixième Exposition Annuelle, Académie Royale des Arts du Canada,* January 30–February 28. (Catalogue)

"Bice sees royal academy as vital force." *London Evening Free Press* (Ontario), 31 January 1970.
"Grande rétrospective de l'Académie royale des arts." *Le Droit* (Ottawa), 31 January 1970, p. 5.
Kritzwiser, Kay. "Hydrant, valve join paintings in National Gallery." *Globe and Mail* (Toronto), 31 January 1970, p. 25.
"L'Académie royale Canadienne des arts célèbre son 90e anniversaire par une exposition à la Galerie nationale." *L'Action-Québec,* 5 February 1970, p. 13.
Ayre, Robert. "Aquarian Academicians." *Montreal Star,* 7 February 1970, sec. Entertainments, p. 8.
"Its time for change, Place for films in Academy of Arts' anniversary exhibition." *Ottawa Citizen,* 7 February 1970, p. 31.

Quebec, Quebec. Société de fiducie prêt et revenu, *Synthèse '70,* May 1970.

"Synthèse '70." *Le Soleil* (Quebec), 27 May 1970, p. 30.

Stratford, Ontario. Rothmans Art Gallery, *Canadians: Crossection '70,* Segments 1–4, June 9–August 31.

Crawford, Lenore. "Stratford show of Quebec artists discouraging in its stodginess." *London Evening Free Press* (Ontario), 3 July 1970.
Fellows, Jo-Ann. "Stratford show has variety." *Kitchener-Waterloo Record* (Ontario), 25 July 1970.
"Third dimension art exhibit at city gallery." *Stratford Beacon-Herald* (Ontario), 8 August 1970.
Crawford, Lenore. "Art show 'Bubbles' with verve, color." *London Free Press* (Ontario), 10 August 1970.

Vancouver, British Columbia. Bau-xi Gallery, *Canadians: Crossection '70,* Segment 1,  June 9–27. (Pamphlet)

Montreal, Quebec. Man and His World/Terre des Hommes, Palais des Arts, *Peinture québécoise 1948–1970,* June 12–September 7. (Catalogue).

Thériault, Normand. "La peinture québécoise revécue à Terre des Hommes." *La Presse* (Montreal), 13 June 1970, p. 42.
"'Les peintres canadiens' à Terre des Hommes." *Le Devoir* (Montreal), 11 July 1970, pp. 10, 16.

Montreal, Quebec. Galerie Godard Lefort, *Canadians: Crossection '70,* Segment 2, June 28–July 18. (Pamphlet)

Toronto, Ontario. Isaacs Gallery, *Canadians: Crossection '70,* Segment 3, July 19–August 8. (Pamphlet)

Toronto, Ontario. Carmen Lamanna Gallery, *Canadians: Crossection '70,* Segment 4, August 9–31. (Pamphlet)

Montreal, Quebec. Musée d'art contemporain, *Concours Artistique du Québec '70,* September 16–October 25, and travel: Quebec, Quebec. Musée du Québec, November 4–29.

"Les Concours Artistiques du Québec et Normand Grégoire." *Le Devoir* (Montreal), 10 September 1970, p. 13.
Roussan, Jacques de. "Le Concours artistiques du Québec." *La Presse* (Montreal), 10 October 1970, sec. Perspective, p. 26.
Lord, Barry. "Le Concours artistique du Québec 1970." *Artscanada,* December 1970, pp. 61–63.
Beaulieu, Michel. "Les Concours Artistiques du Québec." *Vie des Arts* (Montreal), Winter 1970–1971, p. 16.

Toronto, Ontario. Carmen Lamanna Gallery, *Jacques Hurtubise Robin Mackenzie,* October 1970.

Kritzwiser, Kay. "Realism: Springboard to fancy, fantasy." *Globe and Mail* (Toronto), 17 October 1970, p. 32.

1971    Montreal, Quebec. Musée d'art contemporain, *Sept Artistes de Montréal,* March 7–April 18.

Kirkman, Terry and Heviz, Judy. "Seven Montreal Artists: mid-60s works, Show significant as history." *Montreal Star,* 18 March 1971, sec. Entertainments, p. 28.
Thériault, Normand. "Au temps des Plasticiens." *La Presse* (Montreal), 13 March 1971, sec. D, p. 14.

Montreal, Quebec. The Montreal Museum of Fine Arts/Le Musée des beaux-arts de Montréal, *Ninety-first Annual Exhibition, Royal Canadian Academy of Arts/Quatre-vingt-onzième Exposition Annuelle, Académie Royale des Arts du Canada,* March 25–April 25, and travel: Charlottetown, Prince Edward Island. Confederation Centre Art Gallery and Museum, July 1–August 31. (Catalogue)

Kirkman, Terry and Heviz, Judy. "Royal Canadian Academy of Arts, New trends pictured." *Montreal Star,* 26 March 1971, p. 9.
White, Michael. "Art contrasts evident in Academy Show." *Gazette* (Montreal), 26 March 1971, p. 28.
"The cause of the fuss." *Gazette* (Montreal), 1 April 1971, p. 22.
Thériault, Normand. "Un débat académique." *La Presse* (Montreal), 3 April 1971, sec. D, p. 14.
White, Michael. "Academy show shaping up as most controversial," *Gazette* (Montreal), 3 April 1971, p. 46.
"91e exposition du RCA se regarde avec le sourire et un grain de sel." *Le Droit* (Ottawa), 24 April 1971.

Montreal, Quebec. Man and His World/Terre des Hommes, *Expositions Des Créateurs Du Québec,* June 11–September 6, and travel: Quebec, Quebec. Musée du Québec, November 10–December 5. (Catalogue)

Giroux, Jean. "Au Musée du Québec, la Terre tourne et les créateurs." *Le Soleil* (Quebec), 20 November 1971, p. 54.

Montreal, Quebec, Man and His World/Terre des Hommes, Palais des Arts, *Quinze facettes de la peinture canadienne,* June 11–September 6.

Thériault, Normand. "Dans les palais, l'art n'est pas toujours roi." *La Presse* (Montreal), 3 July 1971, sec. D, p. 12.

Hanover, New Hampshire. Hopkins Center Art Galleries, Dartmouth College, *Artists at Dartmouth,* September–October, and travel: Boston, Massachusetts. New City Hall, October 14–30; Montgomery, Alabama. Montgomery Museum, April–May 1972. (Catalogue)

1972    Hanover, New Hampshire. Jaffe-Friede Gallery, Dartmouth College, *Contemporary Art from the College Collection,* August 31–September 10.

1973    St-Georges de Beauce, Quebec. Galerie d'art Benedek-Grenier, Séminaire de St-Georges, *Peintres du Québec,* March 10–18.

"Exposition des peintres du Québec au Séminaire." *L'Eclaireur-Progrès* (St-Georges de Beauce), 7 March 1973.

Montreal, Quebec. Musée d'art contemporain, *Peintres du Québec 1960–1970,* July 3–September 23.

"Peintres du Québec 1960–1970 au Musée d'art contemporain." *Le Devoir* (Montreal), 12 July 1973, p. 11.
Toupin, Gilles. "Petite chronique d'une décennie." *La Presse* (Montreal), 21 July 1973, sec. D, p. 13.
"Peintres du Québec." *Le Devoir* (Montreal), 11 August 1973, p. 14.

1974    Montreal, Quebec. Musée d'art contemporain, *Jeune gravure québécoise,* March 31–April 28.

Toupin, Gilles. "Fleur de lys et wagnérisme." *Le Presse* (Montreal), 6 April 1974, sec. E, p. 20.

Val d'Or, Quebec. Centre culturel de Val d'Or, *Graphisme,* April 17–May 8.

D.R. "Graphisme et graffiti…" *L'Echo* (Val d'Or, Quebec), April 17, 1974, p. 13.

Buffalo, New York. The Members' Gallery, Albright Knox Art Gallery, *Contemporary Canadian Art,* May 19–June 9.

"Canadian art shown in Buffalo." *Montreal Star,* 30 May 1974, sec. B, p. 12.

Montreal, Quebec. Man and His World/Terre des Hommes, Pavillon du Québec, *Les Arts du Québec,* June 20–September 2. (Catalogue)

"Importante rétrospective à TdH." *Le Devoir* (Montreal), 20 June 1974, p. 14.

Montreal, Quebec. Marlborough Godard Gallery, *Group Show,* August 24.

Nixon, Virginia. "Gallery roundup: Checking." *Gazette* (Montreal), 24 August 1974, p. 43.

Hamilton, Ontario. Art Gallery of Hamilton, *9 out of 10 A Survey of Contemporary Canadian Art,* November 8–December 8 and travel: Kitchener, Ontario. Kitchener-Waterloo Art Gallery, January 9–February 2, 1975; Stratford, Ontario. The Gallery Stratford, February 15–March 15. (Catalogue)

Kritzwiser, Kay. "Hamilton's Canadian exhibit uneven but
provocative." *Globe and Mail* (Toronto), 22 November 1974,
p. 14.

1975   Montreal, Quebec. Musée d'art contemporain, *The Canadian
Canvas/Peintres canadiens actuels,* January 16–February 16,
and travel: Quebec, Quebec. Musée du Québec, March
6–30; Edmonton, Alberta. The Edmonton Art Gallery, April
24–May 22; Vancouver, British Columbia. The Vancouver Art
Gallery, June 12–July 10; Saskatoon, Saskatchewan. Mendel
Art Gallery, July 24–August 21; Toronto, Ontario. Art Gallery of
Ontario, September 6–October 11; Halifax, Nova Scotia. Anna
Leonowens Gallery and Dalhousie University Art Gallery,
November 6–December 4; Calgary, Alberta. Alberta College
of Art, January 10–February 7, 1976; Winnipeg, Manitoba.
Winnipeg Art Gallery, February 21–March 21. (Catalogue)

"Time présente onze artistes du Québec." *Le Devoir*
(Montreal), 29 July 1974, p. 10.
Toupin, Gilles. "Une grande exposition de peinture
canadienne est organisée par Time," *La Presse* (Montreal),
1 August 1974, sec. C, p. 2.
Nixon, Virginia. "Time magazine funds museum art." *Gazette*
(Montreal), 17 January 1975, p. 35.
Thériault, Jacques. "Vernissage au MAC, 85 peintures 'pan-
canadiennes.'" *Le Devoir* (Montreal), 17 January 1975, p. 8.
Edinborough, Arnold. "Time counts the years and celebrates
Canada in paintings." *Financial Post* (Toronto), 18 January
1975, p. 12.
Toupin, Gilles. "Une peinture bel et bien vivante!" *La
Presse* (Montreal), 18 January 1975, sec. E, p. 16.
__________. "A l'exposition Time Canada, Le Québec est
négligé." *La Presse* (Montreal), 23 January 1975, sec. B, p. 2.
Gosselin, Claude. "L'expo Time Canada: 'Peintres Canadiens
actuels.'" *Le Devoir* (Montreal), 25 January 1975, sec.
Cahier des arts et lettres, p. 17.
Lehmann, Henry. "On canvas from sea to sea." *Montreal Star,*
25 January 1975, sec. D, p. 6.
James, Geoffrey. "The Canadian Canvas: A Broad Sweep."
*Time* (Canada), January 27, 1975, p. 60.
Walker, Kathleen. "Canadian canvas, A rare view of the na-
tional art scene." *Citizen* (Ottawa), 1 February 1975, p. 64.
Bertos, Rigas. "La Peinture Des 'Peintres Canadiens' Actuels:
Un Chaos Indescriptible!" *Secrets Des Artistes* (Montreal),
8 February 1975, p. 24.
Leblond, Jean-Claude. "Langage nouveau et peintres ac-
tuels." *Le Jour* (Montreal), 11 February 1975, p. 12.
Royer, Jean. "Les chemins exemplaires des peintres cana-
diens et québécois," *Le Soleil* (Quebec), 1 March 1975, sec
D, p. 3.
Boutot, Viateur. "Impressions sur l'exposition Time Canada."
*Le Jour* (Montreal), 25 March 1975, p. 13.

Balkind, Alving; Mackay, Allan; and Saint-Martin, Fernande.
"Peintres Canadiens Actuels." *Ateliers* (Montreal, Musée
d'art contemporain), November 15–February 16, 1975, p. 5.

Brantford, Ontario. Art Gallery of Brant, *Graphex 3, 3rd Annual
Juried Exhibition of Canadian Prints and Drawings with Pur-
chase and "Editions" Awards,* April 10–May 3. (Catalogue)

Montreal, Quebec. *Project 80/Project 80,* Autumn 1975.
(Catalogue)

1976   Montreal, Quebec. Musée d'art contemporain. *Cent-onze
dessins du Québec,* April 1–May 9, and travel: Ottawa,
Ontario. The National Gallery of Canada/Galerie nationale du
Canada, November 1976. (Catalogue)

Bogardi, Georges. "Drawing redefined." *Montreal Star,* 17
April 1976, sec. D, pp. 1, 4.
Toupin, Gilles. "Les cents tournures et pirouettes du dessin
québécois." *La Presse* (Montreal), 17 April 1976, sec. D,
p. 20.
Chandler, John Noël. "Ill dessins du Québec." *Artscanada,*
April–May 1976, pp. 40–48.
Arbec, Jules. "Du dessin...à la bande dessinée." *Le Devoir*
(Montreal), May 1, 1976, p. 18.
Parent, Alain. "Dessins du Québec, Drawings from Quebec."
*Journal* (Ottawa, National Gallery of Canada), November
1976.

Ottawa, Ontario. Institut culturel et social de Vanier, *Group
Show/Exposition de groupe,* April 9–11.

"20 artistes exposent." *Le Droit* (Ottawa), 8 April 1976, p. 36.

Montreal, Quebec. Saidye Bronfman Centre of the YM-YWHA &
NHS/Le Centre Saidye Bronfman du YM-YWHA & HNS,
*Imprint 76,* June 29–August 8, and travel: London, Ontario.
McIntosh Art Gallery, the University of Western Ontario, Sep-
tember 8–October 3; Toronto, Ontario. The Art Gallery of
Ontario, October 16–November 28; Woodstock, Ontario.
Woodstock Public Library and Art Gallery, December; Kitch-
ener, Ontario. Kitchener Art Gallery, February 1977; Oakville,
Ontario. Oakville Public Library and Centennial Gallery,
March; Timmins, Ontario. Timmins Museum Center, May;
Guelph, Ontario. University of Guelph Art Gallery, July; Kings-
ton, Ontario. Agnes Etherington Art Centre, Queen's Univer-
sity, September; St. Catharines, Ontario. Rodman Hall Arts
Center, October. (Catalogue)

Nixon, Virginia. "Artists' panel seeks a new involvement in
printmaker's craft." *Montreal Star,* 10 July 1976, sec. 4,
p. 36.

Malone, Judy. "UWO shows top printmakers," *London Evening Free Press* (Ontario), 10 October 1976.

Montreal, Quebec. Musée d'art contemporain, *Trois générations d'art québécois, 1940–1950–1960,* June 30–August 29. (Catalogue)

Toupin, Gilles. "Musée d'Art contemporain: trente ans d'art Québécois." *La Presse* (Montreal), 1 July 1976, sec. C, p. 2.
__________ . "L'art québécois pris sur le vif." *La Presse* (Montreal), 3 July 1976, sec. D, p. 18.
Bernatchez, Raymond. "Trois générations d'art québécois." *Montréal-Matin,* 9 July 1976, p. 21.
Bogardi, Georges. "1940–1950–1960." *Montreal Star,* 10 July 1976, sec. D, p. 5.
Ireland, Jock. "Quebec art is 'on its head' in Three Generations Show." *Gazette* (Montreal), 10 July 1976, sec. 4, p. 36.
Chapuis, Jacqueline. "Trois générations d'art québécois au Musée d'Art contemporain." *Dimanche-Matin* (Montreal), 11 July 1976, sec. C, p. 15.
"Trois générations d'art," *Le Devoir* (Montreal), 12 July 1976, p. 10.
Bogardi, Georges. "1940–1950–1960." *Montreal Star,* 16 July 1976, sec. D, p. 5.

Montreal, Quebec. Théâtre Maisonneuve, Place des Arts, *Contemporary Quebec Prints/Gravures contemporaines de Québec,* July 1–31. (Catalogue)

Montreal, Quebec. Complexe Desjardins, *Spectrum Canada,* July 5–31. (Catalogue)

Trowell, Ian. "Spectrum Canada." *Artmagazine,* Summer 1976, pp. 38–43.

Montreal, Quebec. Rue Sherbrooke, *Corridart,* Summer. (in collaboration with COJO: Comité Organisateur des Jeux Olympiques).

Dagenais, Angèle. "A visiter 'à pied, à cheval ou en voiture' en période olympique, Corridart, le musée de la rue-musée." *Le Devoir* (Montreal), 10 July 1976, p. 18.
Marsan, Jean-Claude. "Corridart: a-t-on voulu tuer la mémoire?" *Le Devoir* (Montreal), 21 August 1976, p. 20.
Sehmeizer, Elisabeth. "Montreal and Cojo Art Events." *Artmagazine,* Summer 1976, p. 30.

Pescara, Italie. Galeria d'Arte de Pescara, *Exposition de gravures canadiennes,* Summer.

McGee, Mellie. "Exposition d'art Canadien en Italie." *Le Soleil* (Quebec), 30 August 1976, sec. A, p. 12.
"Exposition de gravures canadiennes à Pescara." *La Presse* (Montreal), 1 September 1976, sec. B, p. 1.

Montreal, Quebec. Musée d'art contemporain, *de la figuration à la non-figuration dans l'art québécois,* September 2–October 3. (Catalogue)

Toupin, Gilles. "Deux premières au Musée d'art contemporain." *La Presse* (Montreal), 11 September 1976, sec. C, p. 24.
Leblond, Jean-Claude. "De la figuraiton à la non-figuration." *Le Devoir* (Montreal), 25 September 1976, p. 25.

Montreal, Quebec. Montreal Museum of Fine Arts/Musée des beaux-arts de Montréal. *Forum 76,* September 23–November 7. (Catalogue)

Toupin, Gilles. "Un premier poussin au Musée des beaux-arts." *La Presse* (Montreal), 12 February 1976, sec. B, p. 2.
Bogardi, Georges. "Forum 76." *Montreal Star,* 2 October 1976, sec. D, p. 22.
Toupin, Gilles. "Forum 76: laisser la proie pour l'ombre." *La Presse* (Montreal), 2 October 1976, sec. D, p. 22.
Leblond, Jean-Claude. "Forum 76 au Musée des beaux-arts: des hauts et des bas." *Le Devoir* (Montreal), 9 October 1976, p. 17.

1977　Sherbrooke, Quebec. Centre Culturel, Université de Sherbrooke, *Concours d'art graphique québécois,* June 18–August 25. (Catalogue)

"L'U. de Sherbrooke présente un concours d'art graphique." *Le Devoir* (Montreal), 15 January 1977, p. 8.
Leblond, Jean-Claude. "A voir également." *Le Devoir* (Montreal), 16 July 1977, p. 14.

Montreal, Quebec. Les rues de Montréal, *L'art dans la rue,* August.

Dagenais, Angèle. "L'Art sur panneaux-réclames." *Le Devoir* (Montreal), 29 July 1977, p. 8.
Mathieu, Monique. "L'Art descend dans la rue." *Montréal-Matin,* 9 August 1977, p. 9.
"Des oeuvres sur panneaux-réclame." *Le Soleil* (Quebec), 12 August 1977, sec. A, p. 9.
Rosshandler, Leo. "Du musée…à l'art dans la rue." *La Presse* (Montreal), 2 September 1977, sec. D, p. 18.
Brunet-Weinmann, Monique. "L'Art Dans La Rue Et L'Art De La Rue." *Vie Des Arts* (Montreal), Winter 1977–1978, p. 5.

Montreal, Quebec. Musée d'art contemporain, *Tendances de l'abstraction lyrique,* September 18–October 23.

1978　Montreal, Quebec. Musée d'art contemporain, *Tendances de l'expressionnisme abstrait,* May 18–June 18.

Montreal, Quebec. Montreal Museum of Fine Arts/Musée des beaux-arts de Montréal, *Tableaux de la Collection CIL d'oeuvres d'art,* May 19–June 18. (Catalogue)

Leblond, Jean-Claude. "L'enterprise privée et l'art." *Le Devoir* (Montreal), 27 May 1978, p. 39.

Quebec, Quebec. Galerie Jolliet, *Nouvelle Adresse,* September 21–October 21.

Montreal, Quebec, Musée d'art contemporain, *Tendances Actuelles au Québec, Peintures et Gravures,* November 9–December 10.

"Tendances Actuelles." *Le Devoir* (Montreal), 9 November 1978, p. 22.
Toupin, Gilles. "Tendances Actuelles ou la peinture rétro." *La Presse* (Montreal), 25 November 1978, sec. D, p. 22.
Viau, René. "Tendances Actuelles: un panorama exhaustif?" *Le Devoir* (Montreal), 25 November 1978, p. 23
Martel, Richard. "'Tendances actuelles': Ignorance ou mensonge." *Le Devoir* (Montreal), 9 December 1978, p. 16.
Viau, René. "Tendances actuelles: 2ème et dernier volet." *Le Devoir* (Montreal), 30 December 1978, p. 16.
Payant, René. "La Peinture." *Ateliers* (Montreal), April–May 1979, pp. 2–3.

1979   Montreal, Quebec. Musée d'art contemporain, *Acquisitions récentes,* March 8–April 22.

Birmingham, Alabama. The Birmingham Museum of Art, *The Birmingham Festival of Arts Salutes Canada,* March 29–April 8. (Catalogue)

"Museum to have 3 Canadian exhibits during the Festival." *Birmingham News* (Alabama), 11 March 1979.
Nelson, James R. "Canadian Festival brings an art bonanza to Birmingham." *Birmingham News* (Alabama), 8 April 1979, sec. E, p. 7.

Quebec, Quebec. Galerie Jolliet, *Oeuvres sur papier,* November 21–December 23.

1980   Quebec, Quebec. Galerie Jolliet, *Retrospective 1979–1980,* June 4–21.

LaRochelle, France. La Chapelle du Lycée Fromentin, *Le Symposium de peinture contemporaine du Québec,* June–July.

Viau, René. "LaRochelle renoue avec le Nouveau Monde." *Le Devoir* (Montreal), 30 August, 1980, pp. 14–16.

Quebec, Quebec. Galerie Jolliet, *Galerie Jolliet 1966–1980,* September 1980. (Catalogue)

Payant, René. "Pour Jacques Hurtubise, cette note." *Galerie Joliet 4* (December 1980):n.p.

## Selected Bibliography/Bibliographie Choisie

### Books/Livres

Desaulniers, Louis. *L'Art De La Sérigraphie.* Montreal: Les Presses de l'Université du Québec, 1973, p. 111.

*Dossier de Presse sur les Artistes Canadiens.* Sherbrooke, Quebec: Séminaire de Sherbrooke, 1980, n. p.

Duval, Paul. *Four Decades The Canadian Group of Painters and Their Contemporaries–1939–1970.* Toronto: Clarke, Irwin and Company Limited, 1972, pp. 178–179.

Harper, Russel J. *La peinture au Canada des origines à nos jours.* Quebec: Les Presses de l'université Laval, 1966, p. 385.

Lamy, Laurent. *Jacques Hurtubise.* Montreal: Lidec Inc., 1970.

MacDonald, Colin S. *A Dictionary of Canadian Artists.* 4 vols. Ottawa: Canadian Paperbacks, 1968, vol. 2, pp. 495–496.

Musée du Québec. *Le Musée du Québec.* Quebec: Ministère des Affaires Culturelles, 1978, p. 125.

Ostiguy, Jean-René. *Un siècle de peinture canadienne, 1870–1970.* Quebec: Les Presses de l'université Laval, 1971, pp. 61–62, 76–77, 156–158.

Parinaud, André. "Hurtubise," *16 peintres du Québec dans leur milieu.* Montreal: La Vie Des Arts, 1978.

Péloquin, Claude. *Ballade d'Abitibi ou une histoire d'amour.* Montreal: Editions Michel Nantel Inc., 1974.

Robert, Guy. *L'Art Au Québec Depuis 1940.* Montreal: Les éditions La Presse, 1973, pp. 126, 146–148, 313.

__________ . *école de Montréal, situation et tendances/situation and trends.* Bruges, Belgium: Presses Saint-Augustin, 1964, p. 48.

__________ . *La Peinture au Québec depuis ses origines.* Montreal: Iconia, 1978, pp. 105, 131, 135, 150.

The Roundstone Council for the Arts. *Canadian artists in exhibition/artistes canadiens: expositions 1972–73.* Toronto: Herzig Somerville Limited, 1973, p. 98.

Saint-Martin, Fernande. *La galerie d'art aujourd'hui.* Quebec: Ministère des Affaires Culturelles du Quebec, 1974.

Townsend, William. *Canadian Art Today.* London: Studio International, 1970, pp. 88, 110.

Trépanier, Jean. *Cent peintres du Québec.* Montreal: Editions Hurtubise HMH, Limitée, 1980, p. 97.

### Articles

"Alison Hymas/Imperial life." *Canadian Interior* (Toronto), June 1968, pp. 34–35.

Boutot, Viateur. "Jacques Hurtubise: rigueur et spontanéité." *Le Jour* (Montreal), 7 June 1975, p. 16.

Bongartz, Roy. "Banking art in Ottawa." *Art News,* April 1977, pp. 80–82.

"Collection de gravures." *Rapport annual, 1971 La Banque Provinciale du Canada.* Montreal: La Banque Provinciale du Canada, 1971, p. 28.

Desrosiers, Pierre. "Fusion des arts." *Culture Vivante* (Montreal), No. 5 (1967), pp. 86–90.

Gagnon, François. "La jeune peinture au Québec." *Revue d'esthétique* (Paris), July–September 1969, pp. 262–274.

Hénault, Gilles. "L'art contemporain à son musée." *Culture Vivante* (Montreal), No. 10, Spring 1968, p. 14.

Hudson, Andrew. "Phenomenon: Colour Painting in Montreal." *Canada Art,* November 1964, pp. 358–361.

Jasmin, Claude. Responses to a questionnaire sent to Guido Molinari, Claude Tousignant, and Jacques Hurtubise. Montreal, Quebec, May 1965. (Typewritten).

Lamy, Laurent. "Hurtubise peintre de la clarté violente." *Vie Des Arts* (Montreal), Summer 1970, pp. 18–19.

__________. "Les Arts plastiques 1966." *Le Devoir* (Montreal), 7 January 1967, p. 15.

__________. "Petit bilan des arts plastiques à Montréal durant l'année 1962." *Le Devoir* (Montreal), 5 January 1963, p. 10.

Lefèvre, Germain. "L'art québécois contemporain au Musée." *Vie Des Arts* (Montreal), Spring 1976, pp. 39–44.

Levin, Ray. "Olympic Poster Art." *Artmagazine* (Toronto), Summer 1976, pp. 8–12.

Mardsen, Joanna Woods. "Expositions Internationales." *Vie Des Arts* (Montreal), Spring 1970, pp. 61–63.

McConathy, Dale. "The Art Bank effect, 'Premier Cru/The Art Bank Collection.'" *Artscanada,* Autumn 1975, pp. 30–34.

__________. "Art Bank 'Some sculpture in Art Bank.'" *Artscanada,* Autumn 1975, p. 16.

__________. "The Patron Politicians 'Québec.'" *Artscanada,* Autumn 1975, p. 71.

Millet, Robert. "Jacques Hurtubise: Je peins, donc je suis." *Le Magazine Maclean* (Montreal), February 1969, p. 55.

Ostiguy, Jean-René. "L'âge Nouveau De La Peinture Canadienne." *Vie des Arts* (Montreal), Autumn 1966, pp. 18–25.

__________. "Jeune Peinture Au Canada." *Oeil,* April 1967, pp. 36–39, 49.

__________. "Parmi Les Récentes Acquisitions." *Vie Des Arts* (Montreal), Spring 1970, pp. 34–37.

Oxorn, Pearl. "Airports of delight." *Ottawa Journal.* 25 March 1978.

Pelletier, Pierre. "L'estampe québécoise, ou...l'Amérique en multiples." *Le Droit* (Ottawa), 12 March 1977, p. 20.

Saucier, Pierre. "Jeunes artistes au travail, 'Jacques Hurtubise,'" *Vie Des Arts* (Montreal), Spring 1966, pp. 37–41.

Théberge, Pierre, and Corbeil, Danielle. "Jacques Hurtubise Rétrospective d'Atelier." Interview with the artist, Montreal, Quebec, July 1967. (Typewritten).

Thibaudeau, Claude. "Jacques Hurtubise, Cerfs-volants." *Artscanada,* July–August 1976, p. 49.

Toupin, Gilles. "L'art québécois à la croisée des chemins." *La Presse* (Montreal), 15 November 1975, sec. D, p. 22.

__________. "Si vous passez par la Maison de Radio-Canada." *La Presse* (Montreal), 26 January 1974, sec. D, p. 7.

Tourangeau, Lise. "Jacques Hurtubise—laboureur de couleurs." *Contact CIL* (Montreal), 13 January 1975, p. 3.

Viau, René. "Des peintres dans leur milieu." *Le Devoir* (Montreal), 11 November 1978, p. 30.

__________. "Hurtubise: une peinture qui a du souffle." *Le Devoir* (Montreal), 11 November 1978, p. 30.

White, Michael. "Plasticiens, photos and 1%." *Gazette* (Montreal), 10 February 1973, p. 48.

**Exhibition Catalogues/Catalogues d'Expositions**

Andersen, Wayne V. *The MIT Art Collection.* Cambridge: Massachusetts Institute of Technology, 1968.

Art Gallery of Hamilton. *89E Exposition Annuelle/Eighty-Ninth Annual Exhibition Royal Canadian Academy of Arts.* Hamilton, Ontario: Art Gallery of Hamilton, 1968.

Balkind, Alvin; Mackay, Allan; Saint-Martin, Fernande; Shadbolt, Doris; and Wilkin, Karen. *The Canadian Canvas/Peintres canadiens actuels.* Toronto, Ontario: Time Canada Ltd., 1974.

Barras, Henri. *Grands Formats.* Montreal, Quebec: Musée d'art contemporain, 1970.

Bau-Xi Gallery. *Canadians: Crossection '70,* Segment 1. Vancouver, British Columbia: Bau-Xi Gallery, 1970. (Pamphlet)

Belshaw, Linda. *Graphex 3.* Brantford, Ontario: Art Gallery of Brant, 1975.

Blom, Willem A. *O Canadá em São Paulo 1965/Canada at São Paulo 1965/Le Canada à São Paulo 1965.* Ottawa, Ontario: The National Gallery of Canada/Galerie nationale du Canada, 1965.

Blouin, Anne-Marie. *de la figuration à la non-figuration dans l'art québécois.* Montreal, Quebec: Musée d'art contemporain, 1976.

Boggs, Jean Sutherland. *Canada-Art d'Aujourd'hui.* Ottawa, Ontario: The National Gallery of Canada/Galerie nationale du Canada, 1968.

Boulanger, Rolland. *Peinture Vivante Du Québec 1966 Vingt-Cinq ans De Liberation De L'oeil Et Du Geste.* Quebec, Quebec: Musée du Québec, 1966.

Carmen Lamanna Gallery. *Canadians: Crossection '70,* Segment 4. Toronto, Ontario: Carmen Lamanna Gallery, 1970. (Pamphlet)

Carter, David G. *82nd Annual Spring Exhibition/82ème Salon Annuel du printemps.* Montreal, Quebec: Montreal Museum of Fine Arts/ Musée des beaux-arts de Montréal, 1965.

Comfort, Charles F. *Canadian Water Colours, Drawings and Prints 1964./Aquarelles, estampes et dessins canadiens 1964.* Ottawa, Ontario: The National Gallery of Canada/Galerie nationale du Canada, 1964.

Crevier, Richard. *Jacques Hurtubise.* Montreal, Quebec: Galerie du Siècle, Inc. 1966. (Pamphlet)

Cumming, Glen E. *9 out of 10 A Survey of Contemporary Canadian Art.* Hamilton, Ontario: Art Gallery of Hamilton, 1974.

*10 Peintres Du Québec.* Quebec, Quebec: Ministère Des Affaires Culturelles, 1968.

Eckhardt, Ferdinand. *The Eleventh Winnipeg Show.* Winnipeg, Manitoba: The Winnipeg Art Gallery, 1968.

__________. *The Tenth Winnipeg Show.* Winnipeg, Manitoba: The Winnipeg Art Gallery, 1966.

Farmer, David John. *Canada, The Birmingham Festival of Arts Salutes Canada.* Alabama: The Festival of Arts' Visual Arts Program, 1979.

Galerie Godard Lefort. *Canadians: Crossection '70,* Segment 2. Montreal, Quebec: Galerie Godard Lefort, 1970. (Pamphlet)

Gosselin, Claude. *Projet 80/Project 80*. Montreal, Quebec: Projet 80, 1975.

Harper, Russell J. *5th Biennial Exhibition of Canadian Painting./5e Exposition biennale de la peinture canadienne*. Ottawa, Ontario: The National Gallery of Canada/Galerie nationale du Canada, 1963.

Head, Herbert. *the art gallery in the factory/le musée dans l'usine*. Amsterdam: Peter Stuyvesant Foundation, 1968.

Heller, Jules. *Imprint '76*. Toronto, Ontario: The Print and Drawing Council of Canada, 1976.

Hénault, Gilles. *Panorama de la Peinture Au Québec 1940–1966*. Montreal, Quebec: Musée d'art Contemporain, 1967.

Hubbard, H.R., and Ostiguy, J.R. *Three Hundred Years of Canadian Art/Trois cents ans d'art canadien*. Ottawa, Ontario: The National Gallery of Canada/Galerie nationale du Canada, 1967.

Isaacs Gallery. *Canadians: Crossection '70,* Segment 3. Toronto, Ontario: Isaacs Gallery, 1970. (Phamphlet)

Juneau, André; Saint-Martin, Fernande; and Thibault, Claude. *Les Arts Du Québec*. Quebec, Quebec: Ministère des Affaires culturelles 1974.

Karczmar, Natan. *Art Montreal '67, Paintings and Sculptures*. Toronto, Ontario: Dunkelman Gallery, 1967.

Lamy, Laurent. *Hurtubise*. Montreal, Quebec: Canada Council/Conseil des Arts du Canada, 1972.

Letocha, Louise. *Concours d'art graphique québécois*. Sherbrooke, Quebec: Université de Sherbrooke, 1977.

McCullough, N. *Paintings by Young Quebec Artists./Oeuvres de jeunes peintres du Québec*. Ottawa, Ontario: The National Gallery of Canada/Galerie nationale du Canada, 1965.

Murphy, Sean. *Art d'aujourd'hui/Art Today,* Montreal, Quebec: Montreal Museum of Fine Arts/Musée des beaux-arts de Montréal, 1969.

The National Council of Jewish Women of Canada. *Exhibition And Sale Of Works By Leading Canadian Artists From Coast to Coast*. Ottawa, Ontario: The Ottawa Section of the National Council of Jewish Women of Canada, 1969.

The National Gallery of Canada/Galerie nationale du Canada. *Ninetieth Annual Exhibition Royal Canadian Academy of Arts/Quatre-vingt-dixième Exposition Annuelle, Académie Royale Des Arts Du Canada*. Ottawa, Ontario: The National Gallery of Canada/Galerie nationale du Canada, 1970.

Nelles, Ann J. *Spectrum Canada*. Toronto, Ontario: Royal Canadian Academy of Arts/Académie royale des Arts du Canada, 1976.

Ostiguy, Jean-René. *O Canadá em São Paulo 1967/Le Canada à São Paulo 1967/Canada at São Paulo 1967*. Ottawa, Ontario: The National Gallery of Canada/Galerie nationale du Canada, 1967.

Parent, Alain. *Cent-onze dessins du Québec*. Quebec, Quebec: Musée d'art contemporain, 1976.

__________. *Gravures contemporaines du Québec/Contemporary Quebec Prints*. Montreal, Quebec: COJO arts and culture program/Programme Arts et Culture du Cojo, 1976.

Payant, René. *Galerie Jolliet, 1966–1980*. Quebec, Quebec. Galerie Jolliet, 1980.

Pinsky, Alfred. "*The Sir George Williams University Collection of Canadian Art, Acquisitions 1964.*" Montreal, Quebec: Sir George Williams University, 1964.

Queen's University. Agnès Etherington Art Center. *New Trends in Canadian Painting*. Kingston, Ontario: Queen's University: Agnès Etherington Art Center, 1965.

Robert, Guy. *Artistes de Montréal*. Montreal, Quebec: Musée d'art contemporain, 1965.

Rombout, Luke. *The Canada Council Art Bank Catalogue/Conseil des Arts du Canada/Catalogue de la Banque d'oeuvres d'art*. Ottawa, Ontario: Aerotype Services Limited, 1975.

Rosshandler, Leo. *Forum 76*. Montreal, Quebec: Montreal Museum of Fine Arts/Musée des beaux-arts de Montréal, 1976.

Royal Canadian Academy of Arts/Académie royale des Arts du Canada. *Ninety-first Annual Exhibition Royal Canadian Academy of Arts./Quatre-vingt-onzième Exposition Annuelle Académie royale des Arts du Canada*. Thornhill, Ontario: Royal Canadian Academy of Arts/Académie royale des Arts du Canada, 1971.

Saint-Martin, Fernande. *Trois générations d'art québécois, 1940–1950–1960*. Montreal, Quebec: Musée d'art contemporain, 1976.

Seitz, William C. *Seventh Biennial of Canadian Painting/Septième Biennale de la peinture canadienne*. Ottawa, Ontario: The National Gallery of Canada/Galerie nationale du Canada, 1968.

Silcox, David P. *Canada 101 Edinburgh International Festival*. Ottawa, Ontario: Canada Council/Conseil des Arts du Canada, 1968.

Smilie, W. E. *Tableaux de la Collection CIL d'oeuvres d'art*. Montreal, Quebec: Canadian Industries Limited, 1978.

Teyssèdre, Bernard. *Espace dynamique*. Montreal, Quebec: Galerie du Siècle, Inc., 1965. (Pamphlet)

__________. *Seven Montreal Artists*. Cambridge: Massachusetts Institute of Technology Press, 1968.

Thompson, David. *The Canada Council Collection/La collection du Conseil des Arts du Canada*. Ottawa, Ontario: The National Gallery of Canada/Galerie nationale du Canada, 1969.

Thurman, Sue M. *Nine Canadians*. Boston, Massachusetts: Institute of Contemporary Art, 1967.

Townsend, William. *Sixth Biennial Exhibition of Canadian Painting 1965/Sixième Exposition biennale de la peinture canadienne 1965*. Ottawa, Ontario: The National Gallery of Canada/Galerie nationale du Canada, 1965.

Turner, Evan H. *75th Annual Spring Exhibition/75ème Salon Annuel du printemps*. Montreal, Quebec: Montreal Museum of Fine Arts/Musée des beaux-arts de Montréal, 1958.

__________. *77th Annual Spring Exhibition/77ème Salon Annuel du printemps*. Montreal, Quebec: Montreal Museum of Fine Arts/Musee des beaux-arts de Montreal, 1960.

__________. *79th Annual Spring Exhibition/79ème Salon Annuel du printemps*. Montreal, Quebec: Montreal Museum of Fine Arts/Musée des beaux-arts de Montréal, 1962.

__________. *80th Annual Spring Exhibition/80ème Salon Annuel du printemps*. Montreal, Quebec: Montreal Museum of Fine Arts/Musée des beaux-arts de Montréal, 1963.

__________. *81st Annual Spring Exhibition/81ème Salon Annuel du printemps*. Montreal, Quebec: Montreal Museum of Fine Arts/Musée des beaux-arts de Montréal, 1964.

Walter, John A. *Centennial Exhibition of Quebec And Ontario Contemporary Painters 1967*. Kitchener, Ontario: Kitchener Waterloo Art Gallery, 1967.

Withrow, William. *Perspective '67*. Toronto, Ontario: Art Gallery of Ontario, 1967.

Wysocki, Mathew. *Artists at Dartmouth*. Boston, Massachusetts: The Mayor's Office of Cultural Affairs and the Hopkins Center for the Creative and Performing Arts at Dartmouth College, 1971.

Young, Dennis. *Canadian Artists 68/Artistes Canadiens 68*. Toronto, Ontario: Art Gallery of Ontario, 1968.

__________ . *Exposition Des Créateurs Du Québec*. Quebec, Quebec: Ministère des Affaires Culturelles, 1971.

## Biography

Jacques Hurtubise was born in Montreal, Canada in 1939. He attended *Ecole des Beaux-Arts de Montréal,* where he received a BFA in 1960. Following graduation, he was awarded the Max Beckman Foundation Award and lived in New York for eight months. In 1961 he married Monique Colango and began teaching at various schools and universities in Montreal and Ottawa. He now resides in Terrebonne, Quebec, with his wife and devotes his full time to painting./*Jacques Hurtubise est né à Montréal en 1939. Il suivit les cours de l'Ecole des Beaux-Arts de Montréal, et obtint en 1960 son Baccalauréat en Arts. Il reçut ensuite une bourse de la Fondation Max Beckman et put ainsi séjourner huit mois à New York. En 1961, il épousa Monique Colango et se mit à enseigner dans plusieurs écoles et universités de la région de Montréal et d'Ottawa. Il réside maintenant à Terrebonne, dans la province de Québec, avec sa femme, et se consacre à plein temps à la peinture.*

## The Art Museum and Galleries



Color and black and white photography by Gilles Dempsey, Montreal, with the exception of Selected Works No. 16 by Gabor Szilasi, Montreal; No. 26 by Robert Binette, Montreal; and Nos. 27 and 28 by Willy Cadot, Toronto; Exhibition Nos. 1, 11 and 12 by Mark Chamberlain, B. C. Photography, Laguna Beach, California.

This catalogue was designed in Los Angeles by Lilli Cristin. All type set in Helvetica typefaces by RS Typographics. The catalogue was lithographed in an edition of 1,500 on Cameo Book and Cover by Typecraft, Inc., Pasadena.